Ashutosh The Rising
Soldier To Leader

An Inspiration To The Youth

Table of Contents

Ashutosh The Rising
Soldier To Leader

An Inspiration To The Youth

Ram Nivas Kumar
MA (English, MJMC, MLISc. Dip-In-OA

Ashutosh The Rising
Soldier To Leader
An Inspiration To The Youth
© Ram Nivas Kumar
First published 2022

Preface

It was Monday morning, a cool dry sunny dawn of the day, the eleventh November, 2019. On the spur of a natural instinct, I was pondering over writing a biography on a special character of high social repute, but could not get at the right topic. During the course, I was in high literary pressure. In the evening, it occurred to me hard that I should write the biography of Shri Ashutosh Kumar, the founder of the *Bhumihar Brahman Ekta Manch Foundation* and the national President of the Rashtriya Jan Jan Party. I immediately dialed him and talked in detail about my thought and mind on the subject and sought his consent to go with the work on him. He okayed and I proceeded. Hence, presentation of this book.

I wrote his biography titled *Ashutosh The Rising Soldier to Leader* to bridge the communication gap that the vested interests here conspired to create between the toiling people and the one, i.e. Shri Ashutosh Kumar. I have shared his grief, disappointments, successes, failures and happy moments.

The core purpose of this book is to present before readers my attempt to promote, preserve and propagate the hallowed ideals of a person like Shri Ashutosh Kumar upon which the common folk of Bihar rely.

The views and opinions expressed in this book are of Shri Ashutosh Kumar, the biography is written on. The facts are as reported by him or his near and dear ones which have been verified with his friends, relatives and party workers to the extent possible. The author or publisher is not responsible for any misgiving or misinformation furnished to him.

I own a debt of gratitude to who wrote the Foreword to this book. I am highly grateful to who spared his valuable time and wrote the Introduction to this book to bring it up right to the largest group of readers. I am thankful to Shri Pawan Kumar Singh, Correspondent to

All India Radio, Government of India, whose inspiration to write this book worked well. Also, thankful to the people, peers and supporters who trusted me and strengthened my resolve to write over a miraculous personality who is fighting against the hidden cobra of ugly policy of ignoring the meritorious over last three decades.

No creation is foolproof or complete. As such, I do not claim this book to be free from human errors and fallacy. I am open to suggestions from readers. I request you to read it and offer your valuable feedback. I feel that your suggestions will add value to the content and quality of the book.

Before publishing, I was at great pains and put a lot of efforts to set everything correct and make the book error free. However, to err is human. Errors, crept in inadvertently, if any, may please be brought to our notice. Comments and suggestions are most welcome. Hope the book shall be admired like the sun after cold wintry days and grabbed like hot cakes.

—Ram Nivas Kumar

Before Writing This Biography

An autobiography is a self-written account of one's life. It is a story of a person's life written by that person. *My Country My Life* is an autobiographical book by L. K. Advani. *Indomitable* is the autobiography by Arundhati Bhattacharya, *and My Presidential Years* is a biography of Pranav Mukherjee, the former President of India, written by Ramaswamy Venkataraman.

Biographies are how we learn information about other human being's life. What I wanted to start writing this biography is about an ordinary person, but a big social figure—Shri Ashutosh Kumar. He is an influential family member of the state of Bihar. I know all the important nuggets of him and his family members. I have read and learnt a lot of him. I know him publically out and out. I am aware of his all open positive activities and social doings with their pros and cons that may make this book a good biography.

I have examined all his life's events, relationships and his influence on society. I have dived deep into the writing of this biography, reviewed it until it reaches its finest illuminating touch. The book speaks aloud of him and his everything. It suggests you strongly something anew.

Before going to start writing this book, I asked him the subject for permission. No sooner did I put him my literary idea of writing a book on him, he okayed it with a great pleasure of mind. Then, I looked for primary sources about the subject. I conducted a series of serious interviews related to the subject. I visited several locations that were important to mention. This and all was done for the subject to get at the truth and find facts for justifying the book with its subtitle making a good history in the name.

I visited the addresses where many decisions or breakthrough in his life were made. I remained in the constant touch of his family members and other close relatives residing in different parts of the state for knowing his childhood pranks and getting family details. I also consulted his several fast friends for knowing the true facts of the events and verifying other related factors.

I also studied the time and place of the subject. I contextualized the subject's life by looking past what period he grew up in as well as the history of the places where he lived. I made research on the economics, politics and culture of his time and locations. I looked at the news events happening in the places where he along with his family members lived and worked. This all gave me a sense of how the subject might have the facts that helped me write more effectively. Hope the general readers would accede to the facts in reality and enjoy reading this book at most.

As always there is a context. When I began working on this book, the compelling nature of the subject was so clean. Shri Ashutosh

Kumar is both a complex as well as a simple man, but from within he bears a multi-layer personality. He can be decisive, firm, unyielding and unflinching. And yet, he has a cool and calm temperament that enables him to surmount crisis with dispassionate meticulousness, and even detachment. He is open-minded. During an interview he said, "We open our doors for those who are in need." Though I never travelled with him on his campaign rallies, I interviewed him over three weeks and observed him closely as I had to go on my work on him.

Though gregarious in private, Ashutosh did not grant interviews often where he is and what he is doing. It is possibly the first time he granted such access to any journalist or author, Indian or foreign. In his voluminous oral conversations I had with him, he revealed for the first time such details about his early life and the most controversial periods in his socio-political career.

I have my own purpose, perhaps of your all, to make other people aware of him. My intent behind writing this book is to get the people of Bihar aware of the things that Shri Ashutosh Kumar is doing in their interest. Once the book is published and gets out, and I share it with others, the readers can do with it what they feel most. It's fun for me to hear from the other. I want to know what others feel, and how they take from what I've written. We all have different perspectives and that's what makes this biography beautiful, and helps it to be grabbed like hot cakes.

—Ram Nivas Kumar

About the Book

The book *Ashutosh The Rising Soldier to Leader* is the journey of India's most struggling political leader of this time. He is the supremo of a newly established and statutorily registered political party, the *RJJP*. He is widely known for his charismatic call to the *Savarnas* and his rising popularity among other castes.

The book tells us the story of his life, his entry into the armed forces and beginning of a benign political journey. It begins with his humble origins in the district of Jehanabad (now Arwal) and goes fast to his remarkable rise as a national figure. With the various twists and turns; and the highs and lows, his life is slowly becoming the nation's history. That's why a humble presentation of this political biography.

Well, a political biography is a significant work to understand the evolution to the politics of that particular personality. This book is a significant work to understand the socio-political movements of ShriAshutosh Kumar and his party in the interest of the general people, especially the *Savarnas* and other depressed classes. The book takes you through the journey of Shri Ashutosh Kumar and his unique way of addressing the audience which made him the most favorite, excluded the evil and the jealous ones. If you belong to Bihar and politics incites you, then it would be the best pick.

This book is an attempt to place before the readers the challenges that Shri Ashutosh Kumar is encountering right from his beginning. During his life, he seeks to explain the way in which he handled the situations. He narrates that he always keeps distance from tricky solutions to win over the trust of the general public and a group of political leaders from a spectrum of differing ideologies. This book is not just his story. It is an account of his life leading and sharing with millions of oppressed people, especially in the state of Bihar.

This book is about the present situation in which some people are disappointed with the present governing system that Shri Ashutosh Kumar has been struggling against, for the annihilation of the cause of dissatisfaction prevailing amongst the people of upper castes in India. In recent months, after he was appointed the RJJP national President, observations came under close scrutiny. Adverse things began to crop up. I have carefully examined every bit of them and many more to get at the fact and found them all to be null and void. I did not consider them proper to include in the book.

The book contains twenty-nine chapters ranging from his brief history to his varied views and thoughts on different topics—all that general public would like to know. All the facts and figures are approved by Shri Ashutosh Kumar upon which the work is accomplished. The theme and thoughts, views and opinions, expressed in this book, are of the person this biography is written on. And the facts are the same as reported by him or his close ones which have been partially verified to the extent possible. The author is in no way liable for any variation. But certainly, he is liable for the errors in grammar, composition, punctuation, and the transliteration of the facts into English, and creating true picture of the scene. Any variation or differentiation of whatsoever type shall be deemed to be a matter of human error. We know—to err is human, forgive divine.

The biography of Shri Ashutosh Kumar makes a fascinating read. It depicts his life of immense struggle, adventure and enterprise. The people of Bihar have the privilege of having him as a popular well-wisher. His story is an incisive and remarkably candid memoir.

The book must be read by his party officers, members, followers, and by those who are interested in having a peep into the life of a highly up-surging charismatic political personality like Shri Ashutosh Kumar in Indian sub-continent.

—Ram Nivas Kumar

Reasons to Read

Autobiography of a famous personality might be more of a self-help book than a simple account of someone's life. There are times in our lives when we get disheartened, and we need an external source of inspiration. During such times, one can take help from the autobiography that tells us the real life stories of people and incidents.

Reading about other peoples' diverse viewpoints and life experiences can serve as an additional source of motivation and inspiration. It helps when you choose to be inspired by top autobiographies of influential personalities. India has produced several famous personalities that have excelled in their fields. These Indian personalities have battled against all odds and have reached the pinnacle of success by their courage, determination and perseverance. Their lives have inspired the whole generation of Indians and even continue to inspire people all around the world. One of them is Shri Ashutosh Kumar, *the Son of the Soil* of Bihar.

Well, Shri Ashutosh Kumar is a passionate politician and aspiring social activist. He wants his dream to chase him. He does not believe in "The sky is the limit". Instead, he believes that you can go beyond the sky if you are adamant.

The major reason of reading this biography is to get inspired by real life incidents of Ashutosh Kumar, and get a better perspective towards social and political life. Our life is enriched due to the hardships that occur our way, and the lessons they impart must be learnt at all. Such is the theme with Ashutosh Kumar that I have attempted to enunciate in this book. The book is a handy instrument to crack all essential issues related to the national President of the RJJP. The book is an attempt to know the real life situation of the so-called backward class people and the deteriorating condition of the upper castes people, and to place it before the general readers to know it full well.

The party activists, members, followers and his well-wishers and all those having affection to him have good reasons to read this at most. Hope the e-version of this book will go on a long drive ofdownloading from Amazon Kindle, and the print book will be picked up as one of the sweetest things.

—Ram Nivas Kumar

Foreword

This book is about the life of one of Bihar's most popular, compelling and up-surging personality—a new rising star in the sky of Bihar polity—all of what makes it a unique and fascinating story. He is likely to prove an indefatigable champion of social justice for the people who are suffering from unjust practices being made by shrewd politicians. He has been fighting relentlessly for the welfare of the weaker sections of society. He is uncompromisingly fierce in line serving and protecting India's upper class society who are under constant depression for the cause of cruel reservation policy. For the last few years, his perennially growing and shining reputation for being a very effective communicator is well known. He has endeared himself to crores of people in Bihar and neighbouring states. He has endeavoured himself to even his political opponents by his wit and wisdom, excessive physical fatigue and too much of toiling tours to remote boundaries of states in India, especially Bihar.

The book is about a shining personality, who is constantly labouring hard, from the Bihar politics with many twists and turns; with several highs and lows. The book shows many accomplishments or disappointments with several challenges to become the man a leader that he is. Over quite a few years, he has built up a huge admirers as well as an army of critics. But what unites those who stand with him, and those who oppose him, is the acceptance of the fact that he simply cannot be ignored in present politics that he occupies a distinctive place in our public life.

This biography is an engaging and informative chronicle of the life and time of a man named Ashutosh Kumar, who is round the clock pondering over the cause of depression for the *Savarnas* and dilapidating condition of other categories of poor fellows. He is not only living through recent history, but also decisively shaping it in so many ways.

This book is not a simple biography. It is more than mere an account of a person's life with his clever ideas and brilliant thoughts on several nagging topics. The author has endeavoured hard to know of him and his ideas which he uses during his political activities with supremacy. Everything that the author has written in this book is precisely accurate, interesting and engaging. Hope readers from all corners, irrespective of caste or community, would take much interest in reading this book, and recommend it to their families, friends and relatives.

—Sunil Sharma

Introduction

The book *Ashutosh The Rising Soldier to Leader* is an endearing read with a narrative of the life of Shri Ashutosh Kumar interspersed with his long running strenuous work. The book relies on interviews that were conducted by the author with Ashutosh Kumar, members of his family, close relatives, his juniors and other well-wishers in order to recreate Ashutosh's life and time. It relies on reports and articles that were published in several newspapers, magazine, etc. The book relies on several videos telecast by different media channels. It relies on some letters, essays and notes written especially by Ashutosh Kumar.

The account of Ashutosh's life is based on an extensive research over three years, and marathon interviews with a high range of different people in politics and outside it, for Ashutosh has enabled the author to access his work and life with cloud objectivity. I am brutally honest with my words on his perennial struggle drawing people's affection and the description of the author thereabout.

The book is an unbiased account of the most important figure in Bihar polity today. The author analyzes Shri Ashutosh's values and the people who shared his thinking on him as the special kind of a state level leader.

Personal details of his rise through political risks, his vision of India, especially in terms of the state of Bihar, and his personal philosophy on religion and politics are revealed in this book that is lucid, fast paced, and readable. This being the first edition is a meticulously researched account of Ashutosh's intense and continued campaigning, and hobnobbing with the people of Bihar for the amelioration of their deteriorating condition. The book also includes his thoughts and ideas on different issues that may affect us positively. The book gives a clear vision of next Bihar.

The biography carries credibility as the author has written exactly the same as narrated by Shri Ashutosh Kumar or his near and dear ones. It was important for me to get to know the balance of this book absolutely right. Mutual coordination and understanding matter much. This work is based on reciprocal behaviour and amicable faith imposed on each another. Shri Ashutosh Kumar has been putting the subject of the longest, the most intense and probably the most quarrelsome debating issue that even the highest head denies to participate in. Even the top notch dares not to speak against the current reservation policy. But it is the Ashutosh Kumar, the son of the soil of Bihar, who has the courage to speak so openly against caste based reservation and demands clearly the review of the same keeping in view the poor and pathetic condition of the unreserved categories of people.

Shri Ashutosh Kumar deserves a narrative that the author has presented in this book. The narration is all simple, balanced, objective and fair. It is also unsparingly critical of his daring attitude. I hope this book meets that high standard.

This book is a testimony to what Ashutosh Kumar is known for his clarity of thought. It is a candid reflection of the man, his party, and the next Bihar. In a country where political memoirs, especially on active politicians, are rare, this book is a land mark.

I suggest you all to read this biography because you are the noble children of *Lord Parshurama* and the book is written on a highly ardent devout of Him, we know him by Ashutosh Kumar. Read this biography because you have the blood of the purest source. Read this biography because there is a wound in your every pour. And read this biography because the blood of history never dries.

—Pushkar Narayan Singh

Contents

1. A New Dawn of the Day
2. Ashutosh is Different
3. About Ashutosh Kumar
4. A Bit More

1

A New Dawn of the Day

Shri Ashutosh Kumar was born in Raj Kharasa, a small village in the district of Jehanabad, now a separate district known as Arwal, on the 10th June, 1986. His mother, Smt. Lalmani Devi, the most respected and revered lady of her village, is a cool housewife hailing from a decent Bhumihar Brahmin family. His father is reverentially known as Acharya Love Ji who has been unfurling the saffron flag of Hinduness for over forty years. He is a big scholar of Hindi and Sanskrit. He has high expertise in Astrology. He is a spiritual story teller popularly known as *Katha Vyas.*

His father himself generated his *Janam Kundali.* The *Kundali* showed that the boy might be courageous, adamant and a social worker having high revolutionary insight. It also showed him highly patriotic as well.

ShriNalin Sharma, a strict disciplinarian and cultural Guru of Indian civilization, of the same village was his first teacher who initiated him into the world of letters and numbers. The family executes his religious work under the auspicious words of Katarasin Mahant Swami Ram Prapannacharya J iMaharaj.

Ashutosh belonged to an ordinary family. He received his early education in his village school, Swami Sehjanand Saraswati Vidyalaya, wherein lies a small library where he used to read story books on great heroes. He passed his 10th board examination in 2001. He expresses his childhood days and says:

"My childhood wasn't exactly healthy. So, I dissociated myself from the reality. Looking back, because of all those not-so-happy years, I have a large gap in my memory. The times I do remember are not worth recalling. I didn't know what was happening around me, all that I knew was something wrong. I was restricted a lot and kept in house for fear of terror of naxalism spreading all around in my district area. I was never given an explanation as to who, what and why. News of killing and beheading was travelling afar. Everyone was horror-stricken. My parents kept me mum. They were leading a very fearful life. The laughter in my family was never genuine. The chatter at leisure or around the dinner time was a farce. There was never love in anyone's eyes, words or touch. I was confused and scared a lot."

As the years passed and the boy grew older, his thought towards service to the motherland matured. At a small age of 16 years and 3 months, under the whim of high patriotism towards his nation, he joined the Indian Army on 18 September, 2002 and served for about nine years. During this span, he was posted at Baramula, Kupwada, Rajouri and Poonch sectors in Jammu and Kashmir which were all terrorist torn regions. But a man of working at will wanted some more freedom to work for his own society. He was eager to serve the society in a closer way. Hence, he resigned his service from Indian Army on 13 June, 2011 and started working as a social activist.

Though the man was highly law abiding, he was once charged with a severe case and was arrested and sent to jail for some time. As the case was truly fake, false and concocted, the hon'ble court gave him undoubtedly a big clean chit, and acquitted him of all charges. He was set free. Since then he has been opposing the corrupt politicians of that type Bihar is blamed for.

In the districts of Begusarai and Vaishali, there were several skirmishes between different castes over big chunks of land. Hooligans are always to be made calm down legally either by words or by bullets. It is the persistent hard efforts and strong synchronization of Ashutosh Kumar that it all went peacefully and he solved the problems so easily using his tact and talent.

During Pandemic

There was a big black event in the history of India in 2020, and recurrence of the same more severely in 2021—the pandemic. A shower of deaths and deaths was all around. People were left at the hands of their cruelest fate. The torrential downpour of untimely deaths was rife all around. The countrymen were in high peril, but some politicians remained smiling as if everything is as usual and nothing is to be worry more about. They were indulging in appealing for beating *taali* and *thali,* the whole world was making a mockery of.The exact situation of the time is beyond description. Everyone was house arrested for fear of spread of *sankraman* and getting infected by Corona virus. Countless collapsed. A number of uncountable bodies left to the mercy of the Super Nature. Nobody was there even to wipe out the tears lurking in their eyes. In such a dreadful situation, ShriAshutosh Kumar along with his bosom friends Harendra, Navin, Santosh, Pawan and others were out to serve the sobbing humanity as per extreme possibility and their ultimate capacity. Complying with the Corona guidelines invoked at that time, a big host of companions visited thousands of villages here and there and helped lakhs of needy people at par. They distributed food materials and other life saving essential commodities to the Dalits and other poor people in the slum areas (Dalit tolas) of Nawada, Begusarai, Samastipur and Delhi NCR. Their selfless services shall ever be remembered.

2

Ashutosh is Different

Ashutosh often used to say: "I am different! I was born as a single son in my family where being born a son seemed like God's gift to mankind. That was the beginning of a small and untold story of my childhood. My elder sister was a good and obedient girl. I was also good and obedient in the eyes of the most of ours, but for some a wicked one. They expected me to behave like an introvert, subservient and a meek person, but something inside me was screaming "I am different." Where I always followed the rule book and loved toeing the line, I shirked to be told what to do."

Ashutosh expresses himself: "I felt I have my mind and would do if I think it's correct. Don't think for me. Allow me to think for myself. Allow me to make my mistakes that will teach me not to indulge in similar things the next time. "To trip and fall" is better than never to know how much it hurts after a fall."

That probably was the beginning of "I am different." The tag of defiant slowly began to follow my name.

My Childhood Stories

Story 1

It was the rainy season; the month of September, 1997. At the time, I was a student of class six reading in Modern Academy, Ashok Nagar, Gaya Once I was coming back from my school in the afternoon. I saw a boy, changed name Serthua,throwing a pup into deep water in a nearby pond (pokhara) and making merry of doing that. The boy was a wicked one. He belonged toMahesarYadavand Muneridevi, working aslabourersat a close location in agro-industry. It was a cruel scene. The pup was yelling and struggling to save its life, but the boy was enjoying the pleasure of his dreadful act and laughing at his high hoarse. In the Manusmriti, it is mentioned that all men are not of the same quality. Such type of person is classified in the Shudra category. By swimming anyhow in the overflowing pond (pokhara), the pup came close to the edge, and the cruel heart Serthua threw it again and began to laugh at its peril. He did this several times. In the meanwhile, I came by chance and saw the idiot trying to kill the pup by drowning in deep water. What a heinous act this was! May God not produce such child again! My heart was filled with pity. I was down with tears. I could not stand by the scene. But my heart woke up. Soon a whiff of courage blurred my body. My mind got reshuffled. I was now hell bent upon saving its life. So I took a big risk. Though I was not expert in swimming, I went a long deep intothe water. As soon as the pup came a little close to the edge of the pond, I picked it up so quickly, drew it out of the pond and flew there from in order to save its life.

On the next meet after two days, Serthua began to fight with me putting that incidence afresh. He even tried to hood me hard. First, I made him clear to his heinous act, and then I took him to task a bit more seriously. But he reacted harshlyand I made him understand the thing by giving him some ethical lessons. This should be the best treatment of such type of person, I thought. It was necessary for me to save the life of that little pup. And I succeeded in saving its life. Thanks to God!

After a few days, the same boy (Serthua) was playing hide and seek(a type of rural game) with his friends along a nearby open field. He came running onto a well to drink water and accidently slipped into it. Nobody except me was present there. It was all up to me. Out of nervousness, I shouted aloud and called for some people. Some neighbourersworkingin the nearby vegetable yard came running and drew him out of the well. Thus, his life was saved. I thought—I should not take revenge of his previous evil act, but I should first save his life. It was a scary but the most satisfying event that I played a good role in.

Story 2

The second story of my childhood goes like this: That, I was a student reading in class 10 in New High School, Chandchaura, Gaya. It was the month of Shravan; the English year 2001. The *Rakshabandhan* had closed in. All ditches and ponds were flowing to their full capacity. While I was returning from the school after attending my classes, I saw some friends going deep into the water and trying to pluck the flowers of Bheint/lotus. It was deep water; very risky to go into the pond, particularly for those who do not know how to swim. Instantly, in the right corner of the pond, I saw that an unknown boy had slipped into the pond and was struggling anyhow to come close to the edge of the pond. It was a scary situation. Rumours of his drowning into water travelled fast. He was really drowning and was crying for help to save him, but all the friends fledaway leaving him apart for some type of fear. I was left alone. Though, I was not adept in swimming, I rushed to him taking risk to my life and succeeded in saving his life by extending him my own long trousers. Thanks to God that He helped me save the life of the child! I still could not remember perfectly who that boy was and who his parents were. They say—the child was born of Mehtabi Devi and Kaltukahar.

Story 3

Bhikhari Bind was so poor that he had no money even to spend for cremation and the last rites of his father. He came to my father very early in the morning in that wintry season and asked for some help with money, i.e. Rs. 500/-. Though my father had no money at that time, I asked my mother to break open my clayed bank and give that money to the needy. My mother gave away the money to him whatever small it was. This story touched the whole families in my village. Bhikhari even today reminds that incident and gets obliged. The story shows that Ashutosh is kind-hearted by his nature.

3
About Ashutosh Kumar

ShriAshutosh Kumar is the founder of the *Bhumihar Brahmin EktaManch* Foundation. He is also the founder of a political party named *Rastriya Jan Jan Party*. He is a big social worker and political leader. He is not a private individual. Rather, he is a man of the masses. He is always undeterred by challenges and controversies. He speaks daringly. He does not mince words while addressing his audience or attacking his opponents. His fight is against the unjust. He works for the downtrodden. He even takes care of the feudal clan. He is really working for the uplift of the marginalized and the impoverished people residing anyhow in Indian society, especially in the state of Bihar.

ShriAshutosh Kumar is deemed to be a champion of the social justice in near future who has been fighting relentlessly for the *Savarnas* along with the other weaker sections of society. He is a commentary on recent Bihar politics. He does not go much past back into history. Rather, history itself comes gladly to him. He would be one of India's most influential political stalwarts. He is a new definition of social politics. He is a struggling leader of the fire. He gives one his full support. He carves out his onerous responsibility as I am confident that he will lead the state and wake up to a better Bihar tomorrow.

He has always been influenced by Ram ManoharLohia, Jayaprakash Narayan, Mahatma Gandhi, B. R. Ambedkar, Nelson Mandela, Abraham Lincoln and many more. Whether it's student politics or mainstream politics, he is always guided by inner self. Natural instinct calls upon him every time. His honesty, simplicity and oratory skills are making him a man of mark entirely ranging from a large area of Magadh to the whole Bihar. It is no exaggeration if we say he has touched the height of a national political pole. In the line of service, he amassed.

His appeal and charisma is beyond imagination. He blazes a trail. He brings among us a dash of rustic wit. He is a whiff of hopes and rejuvenation in current dirty politics. He must be a sure cure to the depression of the *Savarnas*. He is throwing upon the earth a big flair into Bihar politics, although essentially a regional leader. His influence has extended beyond his home district. In present political scenario, a few Indian politicians can match the figure of ShriAshutosh Kumar. He is often impacting after impacting important political upheavals and social developments in the state.

He also keeps the ordinary masses at the centre of his narration, because without them he would have been nobody. The general masses too are highly attractive of him for his different moves and toils. He really has the signature of a rustic wit and flair. He is likely to become the CM of Bihar sooner or later. This is no day-dream. No surprise is this. There is no denying the fact as well. Let's see and do the essential for letting our dreams come true.

He idolizes the charisma and methods of Mahatma Gandhi, the simplicity of LalBahadurShastri, the willpower of SardarVallabhbhai Patel, the knowledge of Dr. B. R. Ambedkar, the vision of Pt. JawaharLal Nehru and the honesty of ChaudharyCharan Singh.

His life is dedicated towards the last man of our society. There is hardly anything personal or private in his dictionary. Right from his days as a serviceman in the Indian army till today, he has been doing commendable work and made an impeccable mark for himself. A vast majority of People see him as the future CM of Bihar.

Though he has not attained an old age, he has won the respect and admiration of people from across the political spectrum, including those who are his rivals, while he is still to be a big political polished figure. He had the occasion to work with RJD. The RJD seems to become an alliance partner with RJJP. Though they were fiercely opposed to one another, he managed to do so with aplomb.

His life is dedicated to India's democracy. He himself is responsible for a journey that brought him from the flicker of a lamp in a remote village of *Raj Kharasa* in Arwal to the chandelier of wide range of holistic politics for the cause of the depressed and the deprived people, especially in the state of Bihar. Unity in diversity is our calling card. It is our duty, as citizens, to honour this grand legacy.

Ashutosh is unique. His life is a riveting, insightful and assertive account of his fight to save the right of the downtrodden along with the *Savarnas.*

4

A Bit More

Ashutosh is a harbinger of the upper class people as well as the lower ones. He is treated to be a son of the soil of Bihar. He is a hero emerging from royal Bhumihar family. He is a proven social worker having high perseverance possessing a good leadership quality. He is the founder of the *Bhumihar Brahmin EktaManch foundation*. He is a good red flame of the *Savarna* family in India. Under his apt leadership, a big social revolution is likely to be rife. Inner spiritual power and amazing strength of Lord Parshurama are blurring up in the Indian youth, especially Bhumihar boys and other *Savarna*categories of people. They are ready to riddle the cruel sky over their heads and tear to pieces the land of all evils scrabbling around them. There seems to be a social revolution very soon. Ashutosh used to say—

"*Ham lathi, goliaur jail se darne wale log nahinhain, balkiapneadhikaronkeliyeladne wale log hain.*"(◇◇ ◇◇◇◇, ◇◇◇◇ ◇◇ ◇◇◇ ◇◇ ◇◇◇◇ ◇◇◇◇ ◇◇◇ ◇◇◇◇ ◇◇◇, ◇◇◇◇◇ ◇◇◇◇ ◇◇◇◇◇◇◇◇ ◇◇ ◇◇◇ ◇◇◇◇ ◇◇◇◇ ◇◇◇ ◇◇◇I)The young Ashutosh describes his childhood story like this:

"My life wasn't spectacular. It was all ordinary. I used to love going to river side or large ditches alongside my village every day and play with the pebbles on the bank. My mother was always happy to see all this playing me in the sands.

I didn't understand anything till I was in my late teens. I never even tried to. To me, I was thrown out of heaven or rescued from the depths of the sea. My innocence was strong enough to pierce the thickest of sublime curiosity and nothing seemed strange to me. Sometimes I began to write and draw some lines that appalled my mother.

Also, I liked to read the stories of great revolutionary freedom fighters like Bhagat Singh, Chandrashekhar Azad, Asfaqullah Khan and others along with LalaLajpatRai, BalGangadharTilak and Bipin

Chandra Pal. I also read some crime thrillers and political novels that helped sculpted me into an ardent reader before I was ten. My parents would let me paw through all books and magazines unsupervised because they were unaware I was an eccentric soul trapped in a body desperately longing for an awakening. That's how I got my gift.

I think it also had to do with the day I turned fourteen and through all those years of reading through my parent's stuff, I could realize that books were essentially a tomb of living memories. But I could be neither an intelligent reader nor even an ordinary writer."

He further tells his story adding a little more: "To say it all openly here that my mother was a portrait of untold stories. She was my first canvass; my original inspiration. She had so many secrets and tales, one being the colour of my skin—evidence to a trail where her heart had once treaded to a young girl—being in a conundrum of absurd realities. Once I was in no hurry to find out.

But yet, this was eventually where I would blossom, where I would grow like a lush palm frond on withered soil and as time crawled on, I came to understand and accept that my reality was far from transcend.

5

At a Function in His School

After passing five years of taking leave of his Higher Secondary Education (12th class) from Shakya Muni College, Bodh Gaya in 2004, Ashutosh along with his other classmates from different locations was once invited by his school administration to attend an alumni meet. As he was on leave from Indian Army, he accepted the invitation gladly and attended it upright. It was a small function, but a good opportunity to meet his old friends. He elaborates the story of the day in his classroom:

"When I entered the classroom, on that very day, I looked around at every little detail, many of which I'd probably ignored. Birds were singing in a synchronized melody as they used to fly all around our classroom window. There was the natural aroma of fresh coffee coming from the teacher's lounge next door. My junior classmates were sitting at their usual desk as if they were waiting for the first lesson to begin. It was something different today. And as I entered the classroom, it hit me like an unseen rocket heading towards my heart. All eyes were on me. Someone gave a "sorry"—you had left us while others looked pale. These were my friends. Not just any old friend of course, they felt like family. I grew up with these people. And at that moment as I stared into each of their eyes, I realized something, something which had always been staring back at me. These friends were special.

All the friends and classmates had something that made them unique. And, as they sat there shining like a thousand stars, one of them shined the brightest. She was Fulwatiya (changed name) from my neighbouring location, being neither my friend nor my classmate. She was a new entrant, a fully grown up young lady of over 18. She got dazed at my first sight and went into obsession. She tried to talk to me in tied tongue several times, but I took little interest. Hers was a one-sided love for me. She had a beautiful, bright face and honey sweet lips. She wasblossom soft. She was adorable, amazing, attractive, alluring, affable and affectionate young lady of over eighteen. She was a new definition of beautiful, bold and brainy one. She was full of praise; highly energetic and enthusiastic. She looked to be a female of incredible beauty, grace and charm. She had a long, dark-black and silky hair that covered half of her face, but I knew she'd been crying for me. Her chestnut coloured eyes tried to avoid meeting me, but when she exchanged glances again, I had for her a whole-hearted smile and she returned me the favour. On her second wink I did not think it proper to go with further reply and set her aside completely. We never met again. The rest of that day was full of tears, hugs, a surprise party, games, presents and goodbyes."

Ashutosh says: "Memories of that day will stay with me forever. As supposed, the girl Fulmatiya, had crossed eighteen and wanted to marry a man of her choice. As she was a non-matriculate, she appeared for the matriculation thrice but in vain. She was a young lady of some different caste; mother a laywoman, an illiterate one and father a rude, ill-mannered, thuggish, loutish and philistine type milkman. It's funny to know how a girl of some other caste wants to marry a *Savarna* boy. How two persons of opposite sex having different castes can come so closer and marry each other! In a Bhumihar Brahman family, inter-caste marriage based on one-sided black love is always seen as a low level course of act. Some see it as an obscene affair. So, I bid her a good bye for choosing a better one." This shows Ashutosh's high level character and well-bred *sanskar*imparted to him that every *Savarn*should adopt.

His is a highly arranged social marriage. Thanks to God that He created Ms. Lipi, a prudent one, for him. Her father,ShriVinay Kumar, is a retired army official and mother, Smt. Vimla Devi, a pious lady of high social stature. They were religiously tied together on 21 June, 2003. With all your blessings, ShriAshutosh Kumar and Smt.

LipiKumari are accompanying each other and leading a decent brahminical life.

6

A Soldier in the Indian Army

Ashutosh was a soldier, a brave heart Indian soldier. Under a high whiff of patriotism and a severe sense of service loyalty, he joined Indian Army on 18 September, 2002 and served there for about nine years. But as discussed in the first chapter, he resigned the army and relinquished on 13 June, 2011 not for fear of strenuous work, but for serving the sobbing humanity well at par his inner will. He was a true manifestation of patriotism. He emphasizes the element of love for one's native land. He is now a symbol of true fraternity. His Officers-in-Command always praised him. One of them is Major General Dharmendra Singh Gill who always appreciates me and my work. He used to say, "Whether it is a war or a plain sail in one's life, one must have high patience, perseverance, dedication and constant hard labour to win the match." On the life of a soldier, Ashutoshsays: "Being a soldier is not easy. In fact, it is one of the most challenging things to do. A soldier's life is full of hardships and changes which no ordinary person can face. He spends a great deal of time away from his loved ones. It sometimes disturbs him emotionally."

His Views on Soldiers

Soldiers are one of the greatest assets of a country. They are the guardians of a nation. They protect its citizens at all costs. Moreover, they are a very selfless lot who put the interest of the country above their personal interests. A soldier's job is one of the toughest things to do in the world. They are supposed to meet severe challenges. Their life is very tough. Nonetheless, they always fulfill their duties despite several crucial hardships.

A country sleeps peacefully as the soldiers perform their duties. The first and foremost duty of a soldier is to serve their country without a selfish motive. A person is willing to join the army out of love for his motherland and to protect it. Even though they know they will have to face a number of problems, they still do so for their country.

Furthermore, a soldier safeguards the honour of his country. They do not step back in the face of adversaries, instead they give their best. It does not matter if they have to give even their life for the country. They are acting so happily. He has to do a lot at all time. He is never off duty. Whether he is sleeping in his bunker or standing in the battlefield, he stays vigilant throughout.

Most importantly, a soldier's duty is to maintain peace and harmony in the country. He takes the responsibility of ensuring a safe environment for all in addition to guarding the border. He is always there in case of emergency. They learn how to handle even situation carefully, whether it is a terrorist attack or natural calamity. The local authorities need them to bring the situation under control.

Soldiers have to undergo rigorous training to become fit to fight the battle. It becomes exhausting and physically challenging, but they still go on. To make it work, they do not even get an adequate amount of supply to lead a normal life. Sometimes the food ration is low, the other time they get posted in remote areas without any signal. All this goes not for shortage of ration, money or infrastructure, but as a meter of testing them their reaction.

They also have to make to do in the harshest of weather conditions. They are fighting against all odds. It does not matter if they are searching in chilling cold they have to be out on the battle side. They do not even get enough bullet proof equipment which may keep them safe. But they continue on their work and fight. Thus, we see what a challenging life our soldiers lead to protect our country!

Stories on this Soldier

There are many stories that become legends, and legends deserve to be told over and over again. There are stories of sacrifice, courage, devotion, passion and love. There are stories of real heroes who gave their lives to protect ours. The soldiers are portraying the real meaning of bravery. And their stories become an inspiration to so many youngsters. These soldiers are making sure that the country stay united and the Tiranga keeps on flagging with the wind high in the sky.

There are some stories of brave soldiers which will definitely fill your heart with pride. There will be an instant realization that freedom does not come for free. There are men in uniform sweating their blood to ensure that we could spend our nights peacefully.

ShriAshutosh Kumar was a soldier (now active in social service) who remained posted mainly in terrorist-torn regions. The heart of enemy was always filled with fear as this single man was equal to a battalion for them. He was not only a die-hard soldier, but also a sharply witted personality. He formed a strategy to keep the array under illusion. This soldier was always decided to shoot himself before the enemies could lay their cruel hands on him. The enemy was amazed by his selfless act of heroism. The courage he had shown was extraordinary.

Security is a matter of high concern. The exact elaboration of the duties performed and acts executed by this soldier, ShriAshutosh Kumar, cannot be described in toto for the reasons of safety and security of army establishments and the nation in whole.

Ashutosh is remembered for the unbeaten spirit of Indian forces. He was a lion to the Indian army. He always held his head high with only one aim, i.e. to upkeep the unity, integrity and sovereignty of the nation intact. Jai Hind!

7

Message to the Youth Joining Indian Army

Ashutosh an Indian Army hero gives special messages to the youth of India willing to join Indian army. He exhorts the Indian youth and speaks as such:

Never talk of your duties performed and acts executed in detail elaborating the exact locations in general public. Avoid tactfully if asked about.

Despite rough weather, be ready to be ordered to move and cover the area in which the movements of the militant were last seen.

Be well aware that your life is at high stake. Death is always standing ahead you.

Be always ready to succumb to your injuries.

A soldier never dies in vain. His death is always out of ordinary. Every soldier knows that there is a bullet waiting for his blood. Feel proud to take it for your nation.

No bullet can break the spirit of Indian soldiers. No bullet can stop Indian Army standing against the enemy.

Martyrs always live in your hearts. Story of a soldier passes as a legacy to the next generation. The countrymen are grateful to all the soldiers who fought for us and for our freedom. Always have a sense of combat and feel of modesty.

8

A Mixture of Success and Failure

When things go wrong, don't go with them. —Elvis Presley

What could life be if we had no courage to attend? —Vincent Van Gogh

Do it big. Do it right. And do it with style. —Fred Astaire

A cautionary tale: In his life, he was a failure. He worked hard continuously to overcome his failure and did not give in. Now, his work began to garner intense, critical and financial success. He is incredibly prolific.

Ashutosh Kumar did not start out a success. But he did start early. He was in his mid-teens. He had some measure of success and began to work in politics. He was not an instant success there either, but slowly began to sui a reputation and a degree of success. If Lincoln had quit when the going got tough, the world might be very different.

As a young man, Ashutosh entered in military service as a combatised soldier, but left the job so early for the cause of our society. His real rise to national prominence could also be viewed as a failure.

Ashutosh Kumar is the perfect example that success can come to anyone at any time. He does not want to make pool of money. He battled depression over the brutal murders of ShriRajo Singh, MP, Begusarai, Bihar. He says—"Failure means a stripping away." He stopped pretending to himself that he was anything else than what he was. He began to direct all his energy to finishing the only work that mattered for the annihilation of the depression of the *Savarnas*. Had he really succeeded at anything else, he might have never found the determination to succeed in the area where he truly belongs. He was set free because his greatest aim had been redirected towards a big idea. And so the rock bottom became a solid foundation in which he is building a history in his name.

"Your successfulness and happiness lie in you"—Helen Kellen. This quote says a lot about the way we live our life. Everyone looks towards the external sources for success without knowing the key to success in his own selves. It is really important to know that success takes years of hard work and failures. Focusing on positivity is important. At the same time, looking at the bright side of the things is also important. After working for a few years in the Indian army, Ashutosh decided to join politics. He was quite uncertain of the direction his life was headed. An average score let him hopeless. That is when he started taking out consultations from senior guardians in his areas who could guide him and maneuver his career in the right direction. The job in army did not go so well for him and he wanted to know about more options that were available to him. He was looking for some social work that he can do and satiate his life and that is how he came across. He says that a bad score did not mean the end of a rewarding career, and that this hurdle was a blessing in disguise.

He walked into the office of the Indian democracy and started running a good politics in favour of the reservation on economic ground. He was unaware that this decision would change the course of his career trajectory and life. He first won in the attempt when government announced ten per cent reservation for the *Savarnas* based on their economic condition.

He is always a creative person. He always creates beautiful visuals, shares his thoughts, polishes his skills and showcase his style. He did not want to do the same thing over and over again. Our society requires a level of creativity. Today is the time when he is really happy and content with the fact that he got selected in the eyes of the people. There were moments of confusion and fear, but today he feels a sense of belief and contentment that a vast number of people of Bihar are awaiting him. It is important to know that success takes years of hard work and failure.

Ashutosh: A Social Motivator

ShriAshutosh Kumar is a social motivator also. He keeps motivating his fellow workers, villagers and unemployed youths by exhilarating them in different ways. Addressing to a small gathering at Khiraunti, Parwalpur, Nalanda quite a few months ago, he quoted the stories of Steve Jobs and J. K. Rowling who failed several times but succeeded at the end. He quotes:

"Steve Jobs is one of the most famous names in the business community. His story is one of the most inspiring success-stories in the world. Today, everyone knows about his company Apple. Once, one could not believe that the company would achieve such a great height. Steve Jobs was a big visionary who believed in himself and decided to give everything towards building his company. He was adopted by a working couple at the time of his birth. Steve, being the born genius, develops a taste of machines and computer very early in his life. If we look at his education, he received his formal education anyhow. Although he went to college, but quit only after his first semester. He then took up a job, saved up some money and travelled to India. He stayed there for spiritual purposes and returned home after months as a Buddhist and started leading a simple life. Soon after that he started working on a computer project and credited first an Apple product in a garage. This is how the largest IT Company in the world was built. He has created a legacy today. The rock bottom became the solid foundation on which he rebuilt the most inspiring success-story ever. If this does not motivate you, nothing will."

He further quotes to motivate his fellow beings highlighting the importance and role of parents in shaping their children. He puts example of the parents of J. K. Rowling. The parents of J. K. Rowling are responsible for the creation of "Harry Potter" who is the most renowned author of our time. Everyone knows the fantastic world of Harry Potter today, but not everyone knows about the person who brought that world into life. Her book was rejected by twelve publications. But after sometimes it was accepted and published and the rest is history we all know.

Ashutosh presents some motivating quotes to the youth of India. Motivational stories push you forward in life. The motivational story will encourage you to follow your dreams, treat others with kindness, and never give up on yourself. Find the power to change your life and the way you think. He presents:

Laziness won't get you anywhere.

Don't say something you regret out of anger.

Never let one failure from the past hold you back in the future.

Struggling will make you stronger.

Your reaction matters more than what happened to you.

Be kind to others even if it hurts you. Love the haters.

Even though you're damaged, you still have value.

Don't judge others before you know them fully and truly.

Think outside of the box.

Enjoy the moment.

Stop chasing happiness.

Learn from your problems.

You get what you give.

Stop stressing too much.

Don't screw over your friends.

Your good deeds could change the world. Don't let your circumstances change you. Be always in the original.

Do not get too greedy.

As always tell the truth.

Never deceive your party workers.

Love matters more than material items.
Your priorities matter.
Never give up on your dreams.
Focus on the good things in life.

Focus on your mission and keep moving always forward.

He further suggests the youth to read and learn the following pieces of high lessons of great men for their well-being:

1. Quite often when we face hard times, it is inspiring to read the wise quotes of those who have gone through similar difficulties and adversity. The greater is the difficulty, the more glory is in surmounting it. Skillful pilots gain their reputation from storms and tempests. —*Epictetus*

2. Every adversity, every failure and every heartache carries with it the seed of an equivalent or a greater benefit.—*Napoleon Hill*

3. Prosperity is not without many fears and disasters; and adversity is not without comforts and hopes. —*Francis Bacon*

4. The gem cannot be polished without friction, nor man perfected without trials. —*Chinese Proverb*

5. He knows not his own strength who hath not met adversity.—*William Samuel Johnson*

6. We must accept finite disappointment, but we must never lose infinite hope. —*Martin Luther King*

7. Man is fond of counting his troubles, but he does not count his joys. If he counted them up, as he ought to, he would see that every lot has enough happiness provided for it. —*Fyodor Dostoevsky*

8. Things turn out the best for the people who make the best of the way things turn out. —*John Wooden*

9. Hope is important because it can make the present moment less difficult to bear. If we believe that tomorrow will be better, we can bear a hardship today. —*ThichNhatHanh*

10. However mean your life is, meet it and live it; do not shun it and call it hard names. It is not so bad as you are. It looks poorest when you are richest. The fault-finder will find faults even in paradise. Love your life, poor as it is. You may perhaps have some pleasant, thrilling, glorious hours even in a poorhouse. —*Henry David Thoreau*

11. All of us might wish at times that we lived in a more tranquil world, but we don't. And if our times are difficult and perplexing, so are they challenging and filled with opportunity. —*Robert F. Kennedy*

12. I learned there are troubles of more than one kind. Some come from ahead, others come from behind. But I've bought a big bat. I'm all ready, you see. Now my troubles are going to have trouble with me. —*Dr. Seuss*

13. You are today where your thoughts have brought you; you will be tomorrow where your thoughts take you.—*James Allen*

14. There are moments when troubles enter our lives and we can do nothing to avoid them. But they are there for a reason. Only when we have overcome them will we understand why they were there.—*Paulo Coelho*

15. Inside of a ring or outside, it isn't nothing wrong with going down. It's staying down that's wrong. —*Muhammad Ali*

16. Obstacles don't have to stop you. If you run into a wall, don't turn around and give up. Figure out how to climb it, go through it, or work around it. —*Michael Jordan*

17. Success is not final, failure is not fatal: it is the courage to continue that counts.—*Winston Churchill*

18. Most of the important things in the world have been accomplished by people who have kept on trying when there seemed to be no hope at all. —*Dale Carnegie*

19. The ultimate measure of a man is not where he stands in moments of comfort and convenience, but where he stands at times of challenge and controversy. —*Martin Luther King, Jr.*

20. Be miserable. Or motivate yourself. Whatever has to be done, it's always your choice. —*Wayne Dyer*

21. I am not afraid of storms, for I am learning how to sail my ship. —*Louisa May Alcott*

22. New beginnings are often disguised as painful endings. —*Lao Tzu*

23. It is not because things are difficult that we do not dare; it is because we do not dare that they are difficult. —*Seneca*

24. I ask not for a lighter burden, but for broader shoulders. —*Jewish Proverb*

25. Sometimes adversity is what you need to face in order to become successful. —*ZigZiglar*

26. Always remember you are braver than you believe, stronger than you seem, smarter than you think and twice as beautiful as you've ever imagined. —*Dr. Seuss*

27. Very little is needed to make a happy life; it is all within yourself, in your way of thinking. —*Marcus Aurelius*

28. To be optimistic, it feels better. —*Dalai Lama*

29. Your problem isn't the problem. Your reaction is the problem. —*Anonymous*

30. The word 'happy' would lose its meaning if it were not balanced by sadness. —*Carl Jung*

31. All life's battles teach us something, even those we lose. —*Paulo Coelho*

32. It's not the load that breaks you down, it's the way you carry it. —*Lena Horne*

33. The best thing one can do when it's raining is to let it rain.—*Henry Wadsworth Longfellow.*

34. Life is thickly sown with thorns, and I know no other remedy than to pass quickly through them. The longer we

dwell on our misfortunes, the greater is their power to harm us. —*Voltaire*

10
As a Philosopher

ShriAshutosh gives us a lesson that no matter how problematic our life is, the solution is always inside us. Your qualification, your CV is not your life. Life is something more than this. It is a little more difficult and complicated. It is beyond anyone's control. The humanity is, that enables you to survive its vicissitudes. Unlike any other creature on this planet, human beings can learn and understand without having experiences. They can think themselves into other people's places. He refers to the Greek author Plutarch's quote: "What we achieve inwardly will change outer reality." Addressing to his party workers, Ashutosh once delivered, "We don't need magic to transform our world. We carry all the power we need inside ourselves already. We have the power to imagine and create better. As is a take, so is our life."

He who covers and forgives an offense committed unknowingly seeks love. You have to cover that offense if committed at you in mistake. You being the finest clan of people have to forgive the doer. The hurt doesn't belong to you. It didn't originate with you. The offense came from that situation. It belongs to other person. It is not yours unless you take it in. It is only yours to forgive and to cover. The Scripture tells us that offenses will surely come, but it also tells us how to deal with offenses—cover and forgive. The choice is ours. Don't let your life hurt; just get embedded in your heart. He gives his philosophy like this:

1. The first problem of humanity, more than food, is security. Unfortunately, man has been feeling more and more insecure day by day. The fear of war, which to some extent subsided with the disintegration of the USSR, is still lurking in fundamentalism and the growth of mafia gangs. So international cooperation is necessary to check the terrorists and mafia. Further, a more sincere attempt is needed to reduce

the armaments all over the globe.

2. When you open up your religious Scriptures and get into the Word, you're spending time with God and feeding your inner self. Today I encourage you to develop your personal relationship with God on a daily basis. Ask Him to speak to you through His Word and through His Spirit. Make it a habit to strengthen your inner self because that's how your life will be transformed. You'll discover renewed vitality because of the power of God in your soul. This makes all the differences.

3. God wants to help you accomplish your dreams and overcome your obstacles. He wants to amaze you with His goodness and mercy. We should wake up every morning with the attitude, "I can't wait to see what God is going to do today!" Make room in your heart and mind for what God wants to do in your life.

4. You don't have to figure it all out. God asks you to do is to believe. When you believe, all things are possible. When you believe, doors will open. When you believe, God will take you from the back to the front. Don't let negative labels hold you down. Remember, we serve God who knows no limits! Step with Him and live your life without limits!

5. Prayer for Today: O God! I praise You because You are all-powerful and all-knowing. I ask You to help me take the limits off my life. I let go of old mindsets and negative labels and commit to renew my mind by meditating on Your powerful words. I declare, I am increasing in faith and in the knowledge of Your Word. Thank You for transforming me into Your likeness.

Value of Time

ShriAshutosh Kumar gives value to time. He asks everyone to follow the flow of time. He delivers his philosophic ideas in these words:

"We can catch butterflies, but we cannot catch time. In the far distant future, humans may be able to lengthen their lifespan to live more than 10,000 years, and even then the flow of time cannot be stopped. If time ceases to flow, then our mere existence cannot be realized, because our life processes could not eventuate. The flow of time is always progressive. There is no way to reverse the arrow of time, and that's why one cannot die before his or her birth. It is not possible to clone or reproduce time because any event is intricately woven with time and this neither gets replicated nor could be identified as anything duplicated but has been set to be forever differentiated. Finite time could be enough to realize that anything infinite is unreachable, but even infinite time would not be enough to reach and get back an already experienced moment of time because time flows like an endless river, and there is no boundless holder to freeze time anywhere in existential reality forever. The preciousness of time must be realized by all humans to live on the face of this lovely blue planet in strict duty bounded spirits.

11

A Replica of the Toiling Masses

ShriAshutosh Kumar is a replica of the toiling masses. He is an emblem of a fearless traveller. The journey of his life has been similar to those great men as we study in the history book for high motivation and a lot more inspiration. Though he makes no claim to be anywhere near their structure, it would be foolish of him to do so. Since he started his social and political life that started only a few past years, he has been relentlessly struggling and following the long running adoptable path shown bythe great leaders. He has been unflinchingly fighting against the oppression of the weak, the poor and other backward clan. He has also been fighting for the rights of the minorities including upper castes. He has adopted the call of non-violence given by Gandhi

Jiwhat Mandela, Martin Luther and Ambedkar did in their times. As expected, his path is strewn with thorns, and the journey is not so easy. But he has never flinched from walking down that road. He believes in the dictum—"When the going gets tough, the tough gets going." He is fighting against the most vicious and poisonous policy based on castes. And as such, he is making relentless campaign against it to arouse people's awareness throughout the state and even out thereof to ease the problems and soothe the sufferings of the *Savarnas* as well as the other destitute.

ShriAshutosh is facing the largest coalition of the ugly caste politics. He is hailing from concerted attacks from infamous institutions including Godimedia. He seeks people's support. He is easily accessible without protocols. He wants every member of the society including the downtrodden to have at least a single storey brick-built house of his own. He wants to keep open the gate of all officers for every illiterate and the fearsome fellow. He wants to unlock the ways that are often locked for the rural folks. He thinks that people should enter the public office buildings as owners. He often demands public service as of right. In a nutshell, he fights for the weaker sections of the society. Being a mass leader, having a big view of tremendous social development, he is a semblance of normalcy. May Ashutosh live long!

12

A Fearless Traveller

Ashutosh is a fearless traveller. He follows the dictum that *when the going gets tough, the tough gets going.* He never wants to gag the voice of the oppressed and disallow them the right to live with dignity. He can never allow the radical Hinduism to perpetrate the mayhem on the minorities. He gives the voice and dignity to the struggling masses who live in bondage. This is the reason why people from all corners, irrespective of caste, clan or creed are joining his campaign in huge number. He is really a fearless traveller in the path of social justice and secularism. None can intimidate him.

His life is an open book. He always lives among the people. He has never been a private individual. He has not allowed the walks of bureaucratic or political protocol to hinder him from communication with the people. The toiling masses would never encounter problems in meeting him.

Ashutosh says, "I do not think of problems I may face. I think the manner in which I am travelling on the path of life. I set to begin my innings in this world in a very ordinary environment. It was as ordinary as an ordinary can get. I attended primary school in my village. ShriNalin Sharma of the same village was myinitial teacher. He still guides us. He had a stout bamboo stick to discipline us. He initiated me into the world of letters and numbers. We did not have a cloak to track the time."

Making a good remembrance of his school days, he tells: "While going to school, I often moved to an orchard for plucking some mangoes, plum or even tamarind. Sometimes orchard owner chased me and I fled in, not with the sense of guilt I did, but for enjoying a sense of delight."

Growing up in the sleepy towns of Arwal and Jehanabad, Ashutosh never imagined that one day he would go on to India's largest people's dais of democracy accompanied with crores of people across the country. Indomitable is the story of his life as a sweet-tongue and kind-hearted person, and the challenges he is facing.

Ashutosh's Dedication

His life is dedicated to the whole society in wider context of India. He is committed to resolving the problems of the depressed classes arising out of politically ignoring policies.He is deeply indebted to his parents for allowing him to bloom and work in his way. He is indebted to his wife and sons for their constant endeavour and support in the ways they can. He is grateful tomillions of young Indians who hail from the small villages of India who havestars in their eyes, hopes in their hearts, and belief in their mind that Ashutosh can excel and contribute to building a big dream Bihar.

A Phone Call from Ashutosh

It was a rainy season and I was on a two-day weekend. I got a call from the usual effervescent Ashutosh, requesting me if I would be inclined to read his a brief biographical essay written on a few pages in Hindi. Before I had even made up my mind, his unedited manuscript was in my inbox. As I began to scroll my smart phone, I just wanted to keep reading more. After reading it several times, I made up my mind to include his essay in the biography onthis ever growing big visionary.

My Recognition with Ashutosh

I cannot claim to have known Ashutosh for decades. I first met him in 2014 at Nishchalganj near Ekangarsaraiwhen he was heading towards the hospital at Biharsharifto see and help a patient suffering from some acute diseasse. The next time, I saw him in a *Dalit tola*, the villagers say this *Chamartoli*, in my village named Salalpur under Parwalpur police station, Nalanda where he had visited to address a small gathering of the dalits. I instinctively knew Ashutosh to be a cut above the rest. He is really uprising to make his mark as a popular leader in Indian history. Those who follow his stories more closely never forget to graciously embrace him as a people's leader. The title "People's Leader" never frazzled him. He knows he had to get on with the task, tracking challenges after challenges that confronted him as he has to hem the country's largest democratic set-up.

He steers away from aspiring to be a superman. He does not wallow in guilt for being away from home when work demands it to his credit. He seized every opportunity to help other colleagues.

13

Social Identity of Ashutosh Kumar

A few can imagine this powerful man struggling initially to balance the ledger of people's behaviour or count their heart and mind correctly. He acknowledges the opportunity of standing on the shoulders of giants—from his mentors and supportive colleagues to his family and friends— who always rallied around him whenever he needed.

Standing grounded in a position of threat and danger is always a fierce test of his character. That is why his family, friends and general public are so impressed by him. His anchor remains his inner-self. The humble Ashutosh knows life is true triumph.

He leaves the public with the thoughtful ideas provoking to execute them in reality. Work on the ground is a must. Only hue and cry does not suffice our purpose. A large group of family and friends of the State of Bihar is the beacon light for the big society of hostile Bihar. He continues to live up to the meaning of his name—one who is unstoppable. He is indomitable. His life is the best memoir I have ever read. He is really a trailblazing in a new avatar.

His life is the extraordinary portrayal of one of India's leading political personalities blooming day in day out. He poignantly describes the sense of turmoil in his life during his under-16 that affected time on it and millions of residents of Bihar.

He had not a loving childhood with his parents. He had to see the cruelest scene of naxalism in his area. One of the most horrific periods of human history was the time of eighties. It is a testament to the naxalism that he saw, faced and suffered till long. He continued to persevere and survived in the face of the most adverse of circumference. He survived to keep his story and his memory alive for the rest to the world through the ages. He has conducted countless meetings and rallies and has acquired a national profile. Yet the man remains an enigma. His supporters regard him as a visionary, a decisive leader India needs today. His detractors see him as a polarizing figure. His life is patterned with moments of adversity where the person is working hard and fighting against bigger forces. This is the story of his extraordinary social life.

14

Nine Inner Qualities

Though I have not lived with Ashutosh for long, nor did I move with him so frequently, I tried to know of him from his family members, neighbourers, relatives and friends. What they told about him seem me to be beyond any doubt. Hence, I wanted to include them in this book as an instance to the other fellows. ShriAshutosh has some special inner characteristics much told about which are mentioned point-wise as under:

1. He's smart, full of wit and wisdom.
2. He makes others laugh. He actively supports your career.
3. He makes as much effort with your friends and family as you do with him.
4. He's emotionally intelligent. He maintains overall discipline in his life.
5. He respects your opinions and listens to what you say.
6. He's willing to put the work in so immediately.
7. He celebrates others' achievements.
8. He has high respect for the elders.
9. He is courageous, adamant and patriotic having high revolutionary insight.

If a man has such extra inner qualities, he is sure to be a cut above the rest.

15

The Rashtriya Jan Jan Party

The Rashtriya Jan Jan Party (RJJP) is a newly created political party in India. It is statutorily structured and registered under the Election Commission of India. ShriAshutosh Kumar is the founder of this party. He is also the National President of the RJJP. It first contested the Bihar Assembly Elections, 2020. In a press conference organized in Patna, Ashutosh told that the Rashtriya Jan Jan Party has been formed to achieve golden dreams of Bihar through industrial development. On 18th July 2021, the Party convened a meeting with its supporters to spread party views in Bihar. They cleared their stand that they will stand with all castes and communities. They also shared its slogan *Har-Ek Booth with Five Youth.*

The main ideology of the Rashtriya Jan Jan Party is anti-reservation. It has been vocal in demanding EWS reservation. The party has also been indulged in the relief works of migrants and flood victims. The party has also been conducting membership drives since its inception.

The Rashtriya Jan Jan Party contested almost all those Assembly seats having forward caste dominant population. It gained huge votes from all castes.

During Corona virus pandemic, the party played a major role. One of the intriguing features of the corona virus pandemic is how sharply it has illuminated the importance of effective political leadership. Wherever we stand on the political spectrum, we're looking to elected officials to help steer us through this crisis. And the party stood high at the test.

16

An Accomplished Politician

While I don't want to talk about specific politicians, it is the time to talk to. The time has given me a sense of what makes a good one—as a policy maker, that is, rather than a candidate. One of the ironies of our system is that the skills and attributes that put someone in office are usually not the skills needed for success once they're there. Yet, as a nation, we depend on politicians' ability in office to move us forward.

For starters, I think the most successful politicians have integrity. When you're interacting with many others to deal with complex and difficult public issues, it's hugely important that you can trust someone's word. Most of the politicians I have read stay true to what they tell you. They recognize the need to work with others and know that trust matters. One of them is truly ShriAshutosh Kumar.For the reasons, politicians tend to be skillful at working with all sorts of people. Sizing others up accurately—not just whether they're trustworthy, but the skills and strengths they might bring to a given policy or organizing effort—is vital. So is not rushing to make quick judgments, but instead letting others show through their actions what they can accomplish. Many good politicians are quite tolerant—they know people make mistakes or errors of judgement and that nobody has a monopoly on the truth to perform flawlessly.

One of the best politicians I've read—Ashutosh Kumar comes to mind—also has a way of charming some people who don't agree with him. But he is affable and engaging. He listened carefully to what they (people) had to say. You perhaps would find it difficult to guess he had any idea what they thought of him. Walking out with them, I once asked what they thought about him. They all responded, "We may have some disagreements with him (Ashutosh), but what a nice fellow!"

I've been impressed over the years by the energy and drive to get things done that good politicians bring to their work. When I talk with people who want to get into politics, I usually open the conversation with two questions: What's your energy level? And what your spouse or partner thinks about it? Both are critically important because a campaign might be all-consuming, serving in office is even more so, especially if you're a politician who wants to accomplish change. An unsupportive spouse or partner spells problems down the road.

At the same time, accomplished politicians know how to rein in their enthusiasm and zeal. They practice patience and perseverance and prepare for the long haul, because they understand that controversial things don't get easily done in our system. They believe that facts matter, because they're the starting point for any productive negotiation. And they're very good at managing their time efficiently. In this sense, ShriAshutosh stands atop.He is able to put aside partisan differences when necessary, and work for the common good.

17

A Political Guru

ShriAshutosh Kumar is a political Guru as well. He teaches college students willing to join the RJJP as under:

Be not a politician; be a social worker. Politics can be challenging and rewarding, where you potentially have the power as an elected official to make a difference in your community. To be an effective politician, you will need to combine hard work with smart choices. You will also need to focus on running a successful campaign for office so you can end up in a position of influence and represent voters on a local or national level.

A piece of advice to students joining politics: Though you can get into politics without even having finished your high school, you may be more appealing to voters if you have a relevant degree. An undergraduate degree in Political Science will allow you to have a strong foundation in the basics of government and politics, as well as the history of politics in your country.

Most colleges and universities offer a B.A. in Political Science. A Political Science degree will allow you to understand how to process and analyze political data and strengthen your communication skills. You may also take courses in conflict resolution and public speaking.

Take public speaking classes. If you decide not to pursue a B.A. in Political Science, you should still consider taking public speaking classes. You can take these classes at your local college or university, or through a public speaking association. Public speaking classes can help prepare you for a key element of a successful politician: the ability to speak persuasively and effectively in front of a crowd. This is a good option if you do not want to pursue a B.A. in political science, or if you are looking for a way to improve your political skills during your free time. Taking even a few public speaking classes could help you gain more self-confidence and self-assurance.

Participate in speech and debate. If your high school offers speech and debate classes, you should sign up and push yourself to compete against your peers in debates. Strong debate skills will come in handy for you are having to debate with other candidates on local issues during your campaign.

You may want to compete in foreign competitions through the National Speech and Debate Association to push yourself even further and get better at performing in front of an audience.

Stay updated on the latest politics in your community and nationally. A good politician will be well educated on local events, especially if he is running for local office. Stay on top of the latest political events in your community, from the smallest to the largest issues. You should also be aware of what is going on a national level. So you should be well informed and get in the habit of remembering the latest news events.

One way to do this is to use social media to your advantage, and follow known politicians and individuals involved in politics on big platforms like Twitter and Facebook. You can then read what they are talking about and get information through their news feeds.

You should also get in the habit of checking several political news sites and blogs every day. Try to look at several news sources that present differing opinions on a topic. For example, you may check a conservative news outlet for information on an abortion case, and then a liberal news outlet for information on the same case. This will give you a well rounded sense of both sides of the issue and also help you determine where you stand on the same issue.

Get involved in local community initiatives and causes. Before you run for the President of the United States, you need to start small and work your way up from local politics to national politics. To be effective at a local level, you will need to connect with your community and get involved. You should volunteer for local committees and try to sit on local boards for causes that you are passionate about. Join the local chapter of your preferred political party and get involved in the initiatives for the political party in your community.

Creating a strong presence in your community will alert community members of who you are and what you stand for. Devoting your time to local causes and initiatives will also show your community that you are willing to volunteer your energy out of a need to do some good, not just to get paid. This will become useful latter when you decide to run for office.

You should also reach out to the leaders in your community and connect with them. This will help to set the groundwork for your campaign latter, as you will have these political relationships to lean on when you need them. Forming strong bonds with these leaders will also allow you to learn and watch how these leaders conduct themselves in the community. You should take mental notes and pay attention to how these leaders gain respect and acknowledgement in the community. You can then use these skills latter in your campaign.

Speak at local events and participate in local debates. You should use local events as an opportunity to practice your public speaking skills even if they are not political gatherings. Try to be in the public eye as much as possible, especially for the causes that you are passionate about. You should also participate in local debates as a representative for your community, as this will allow you to showcase your passion for change and your public speaking abilities.

In addition to speaking to large audiences, you should also get into the habit of speaking to individuals in the community one to one. This could be through conversations with locals at coffee shops and local hang outs as well as time spent in the crowds talking to individuals who are participating in local events. This will get you used to connecting with people on a smaller scale and making a personal connection with your potential voters.

Use social media to promote your ideas. In this day and age, having a strong social media presence is essential to maintaining a public persona. You should set up social media accounts for yourself that showcase your public self and use it on a consistent basis to connect to others. Your social media profiles should have professional photographs and you should maintain a persona that is appropriate for someone who may become an elected official one day.

You can use your social media accounts to follow known political figures in your community and nationally. You can also use your social media to build momentum for your political campaign.

Start small and then work your way up. Most successful politicians started at the local level and then worked their way up for the years to national positions at the federal level. If you are just entering politics, you should focus on building momentum as a local politician and then use this as a foundation to aim for higher positions. You may start by campaigning for a school or community board position, a position as a mayor or a town council member, or a seat in the Lower House of the state government.

At the local level, staffs, budget, and campaign funds are usually small and limited. You may not have a lot of funding or a big staff, but you may not need it to be successful at the local level.

Getting a position at the local level can also allow you to build relationships within your preferred political party, which could help your career latter if you decide to go for a higher position in the party.

Outline your platform. To run an effective campaign, you will need to develop your political platform. Your platform should detail where you stand on key issues in your community and how you are going to fulfill the expectations of your elected role.

You may also include a campaign plan along with your platform. The campaign plan may be used internally by your team to ensure the campaign is well planned and laid out ahead of time. The campaign plan may detail the estimated budget of the campaign, your marketing strategy, and your fundraising strategy.

Create a marketing strategy. Effective communication is a major part of a successful campaign. You should sit down with the marketing persons in your team and come up with a detailed marketing strategy. This will allow you to stay connected to your voters and help to promote your platform.

Your marketing strategy may involve creating a campaign website where you have a professional photograph of yours, your campaign slogans, and information about your platform. You may also do daily social media updates to connect with potential voters.

You may also create printed materials like brochures or fliers to put up around the community to promote your campaign.

Solicit funding for your campaign. No matter how small your campaign may be. You will still need funding to run your campaign. These funds will help to pay for your marketing material, your campaign supplies, and any travel you need to do for the campaign.

You should use the lists, labels, and letters approach. Start by creating a list of people for you or the fundraiser volunteers to call. Then, label and send out letters to get solicitations for funds into the hands of potential supporters in your community.

You should also be willing to knock on the doors in the neighbourhood and ask for the support of your voters on Election Day. Hand out brochures and fliers at public, local events to solicit more fundraising for your campaign.

Run an honest, motivated campaign. Remember that most political campaigns, even at the local level, can be challenging and require lots of hard work. You may end up working overtime to try to win the election, and your volunteers may be working with you to get your platform out to as many voters as possible. Though you may be motivated to win, you should also try to run an honest campaign. Make campaign promises that you can keep and strive to work with your community to respond to their needs, rather than serve your own needs or wants. Running an honest, motivated campaign will likely increase your chances of success and your chances of remaining in office once you are elected.

Most politicians are comfortable speaking in front of a crowd and do not mind being scrutinized by the public. A big part of the politician is in the public eye on the daily basis. Extroverts are often more comfortable with this than introverts. But this does not mean an introvert cannot go into politics.

18

Ashutosh on Leadership

Art of leading people, small or big, is leadership. A leader's inner quality, inherent ability, certain traits and special characteristics—all together make him a man of true leadership. Ashutosh throws light on leadership and suggests like this:

Do small projects with people and help talk them through it. Use something you already have your experience in, to project your confidence and ambition to talk.

Do we ever ask—"Who is a good politician"? Somehow, in a country like ours, which is always in election mode, discussions on politics are a common sight at roadside, tea-stalls and on train journeys, but we happen to avoid this question. Most of these discussions have critical undertones. Some are polarized based on the political ideology one assigns to, and mostly about "choosing the lesser evil." So what refrains us from indulging with the real question that matters?

At this juncture, for the survival of a healthy democracy, India could immensely benefit from a research-backed discourse on 'who is a good politician.' It must happen.

People have lapped up the idea that the government keeps the citizens uneducated because it's easier to rule over an uneducated citizenry. But with internet affordability, the barrier to information has been broken and citizens can access information at the touch of their smart phones today. This should have indulged citizens of a country marred by corruption, high crime rates and all things wrong in a developing country, to find the right kind of politicians as their representatives.

A democracy, that aspires to become a superpower and the knowledge hub of the world, has struggled to keep up with the evolving nature of politics. We idolize the first generation of politicians who grew out of the independence struggle against British rule. We idolize the charisma and methods of Gandhi, the simplicity of Shastri, the willpower of Patel, the knowledge of Ambedkar, the honesty of ChaudharyCharan Singh, and so on. We live in nostalgia idolizing leaders of yore, but are unwilling to develop leaders of the future. If only previous governments or at least the political parties had invested to identify suitable candidates to contest elections, the country would have benefitted a whole lot from it. But how do we get there?

The developed countries have reached where they are because they understood the importance of research and have invested in it. We must understand that knowledge is essential to the development of the country. Knowledge of the sustainable mechanism to identify the right kind of candidate for political office would yield promising results. But in India, neither the citizens nor the political parties have worked to initiate a discourse on 'who is a good politician'. Is it a myth or is it actually possible to define the traits of a 'good politician'?

The political parties use several subjective criteria to select candidates for electoral office such as eloquence, intelligence and charisma. They may also select candidates based on ambiguous parameters such as party loyalty, family ties, and so on. The use of proxy variables like 'educational attainment' and 'career path' for measuring eloquence and charisma creates problems because the studies which use these criteria may find it difficult to distinguish between those who gained high social status through the attainment and those who obtained it through privilege.

An ideal candidate good for electoral office is a person who has a genuine and demonstrable knowledge of the issues and problems faced by people, and a dedication to address them. That person should also have outstanding interpersonal skills, and should be able to fight for a cause and negotiate compromises when necessary. It can be deduced that the qualities for a good politician are knowledge, problem-solving attitude, and intention to work for a cause and good communication and advocacy skills.

Organizational psychologists have also contributed to identifying the 'traits of a good politician'. In order to capture common views about the good and bad political performance, they interviewed people from all stakeholder groups to develop a framework of competence and behavioural indicators that could be used as selection criteria for candidates for political office. Voters believe that local candidates may have a better understanding of local issues which may help them in addressing those issues effectively.

Several qualities of a good politician, as outlined by previous research, have a close association with the qualities identified for leadership in various theories of management and social work studies. Thus, leadership qualities such as selflessness, integrity and vision become critical to the definition of a good politician. However, without research-backed indicators for a good politician, it's a different story in the Indian context as politicians are not perceived positively by many people. Some say—"most politicians are corrupt" with more than 50 per cent of the respondents expressing that "no matter who wins elections; things do not change very much."

Research in this direction within the Indian context should consider a multi-dimensional approach taking into account that a politician has multiple roles to play. It should take inspiration from the fields of management, social work and psychology. Such initiatives by political parties would help develop a sustainable mechanism for them to create a pool of suitable candidates for political recruitment.

Focused initiatives must also be taken up by think tanks, civil society organizations and research-oriented academic institutions in India for identifying traits of a good politician from the perspective of the political parties and the voters.

This suggests that we, in India, lack a comprehensive discourse on 'who is a good politician'. At this juncture, for the survival of a healthy democracy, India could immensely benefit from a research-backed discourse on this issue. Political organizations should think of it.

19
Futuristic Vision of Ashutosh Kumar

First of all, we have to keep an open mind to understand the needs of the country. We have entered in the 21st century. And what should be the developmental changes during this century is a matter of prime concern for all of us. ShriAshutosh Kumar has his vision as under:

1. Well, we have a democratic setup of government. And the democratic setup of government has proved to be the best form of government in the 20th century. The 21st century has to put it in practice and see that all the governments in the world behave democratically and there should be no domination, either political or economic.

1. The concept of global village has come into existence in the place of British rule where the sun never set. Development of computers and communication network changed the face of the earth. Distance is not a big problem in this century. Villages should be developed in the same way as towns are being.

1. The fields of Management and commerce are likely to take a pride of place and there is a need to develop man power equipped with appropriate skills. Cross border transformation of goods is needed to develop International trade.

4. Naturalism or returning to nature is also the need of the century. In the name of fashion and civilization, we have been distancing ourselves from nature and natural products. It is not only the nylons on our bodies that are artificial, but our smiles and behaviour too became artificial to some extent. The turn of the herbal products, instead of synthetics, will have to go a long way in the 21st century.

5. The water level is going down gradually at many places and it is said that water may be the cause of wars in future. So conservation of water is also necessary in the line of the conservation of energy sources like diesel and petrol.

Having gone through some of the global needs of the century, now let us look at the needs of India in the new century:

India Needs

1. In India the greatest need of the century is poverty alleviation. This is possible through developments such as Green Revolution or e-commerce. But unfortunately we relied more on subsidizing prices of goods which was unproductive. Adopting modern techniques in water management like—drip irrigation and by developing refrigeration and air conditioning, we can conserve and export our agricultural and horticultural products. If India is to grow into an economic power in the 21st century, we should develop scientific research in pure and applied sciences to aid agriculture and industry, and our exports should grow at least at the pace of our satisfactory level.

2. Developments in the fields of computers and communication systems have given an edge to India over all the other countries in the world. It is a matter of pride that a majority of the computer personnel in the USA are Indians, and a majority among the Indian experts is from Andhra Pradesh, Karnataka, Tamil Nadu and other south Indian states. Though there is a setback to employment of computer personnel in the USA, it is only temporary and only because of recession in the US economy, and not because of any stagnation in the field. Particularly in India, the demand will grow in coming years, according to the estimates of experts in the field. So India needs more and more computer personnel. We should make Bihar a big computer hub and try to produce more computer engineers who may compete with the world at par.

4. Information revolution and things like e-mail, internet, e-governance, and video conferencing have changed the functioning of the government. There is more transparency. But we have made only a beginning and have to go a long way in the years to come. Hardware, too, will have to be developed with software.

5. Certain courses like Fashion Designing, Catering Technology, Refrigeration and Air conditioning, Genetics, Biochemistry, Microbiology, Biotechnology, Medical Transcription, Soft Skills, Advertising, and Modeling have bright prospects compared to traditional courses. Service sector in computers will benefit most that needs to be developed.

6. Fundamentalism and corruption have grown to alarming proportions in India, and lack of serious political will to curb them is the main reason for that growth. Corruption among politicians and officials has become rampant. People in general and particularly those at high places have become so selfish that it is hard to believe that the very same society fought with the British sacrificing their cloths, jobs, careers, etc. under the leadership of Mahatma Gandhi. Writers should create an awareness among public about the state of affairs and make people rededicate themselves for the country to develop it and thereby themselves. The morale of the public should result in good work culture in the new century. Then only politicians will stop politicizing every issue and think about people's welfare.

20

Ashutosh's Views on Better India

Ashutosh has his own views on better India. He has the same consent as that of Prof.Rajendra Singh Baisthakur. He enumerates his opinion as mentioned hereunder:

Civic education is the prime requisite for every Indian. People should be educated about the government functions. They should be educated about how the money, they paid as taxes, is utilized. They should know about the duty of each politician. They should be aware of the duty of each officer in the government so that they can keep watch on their functioning. Thus, they may know who to vote. Then they will not be influenced by money, muscle-power, caste, region, religion, etc. Then they will not elect inefficient, corrupt and criminals as their representatives. That will be the real democracy.

Ashutosh says that no family, society or nation can exist without a definite set of norms created for its own welfare. Existence of all, in our pluralistic society, is possible only with a set of rules to be followed by all. All religious, regional, local customs and practices must be in accordance with the constitution we gave to ourselves. It is the duty of all to see that we follow it. If anyone fails to follow, he should be taken to task by the law enforcing executive and punished by the judiciary. Executive should have a free hand in dealing with law breakers without interference from politicians.

There is an immediate necessity of reforms in our judicial system. Cases going on for long duration make criminals fearless and encourage them to continue their activities. Lawyers need to be trained periodically to interpret law properly. All loopholes to postpone things and repeated appeals have to be closed. Cases relating to politicians, corruption and atrocities on women and weaker sections should be heard in fast track courts with a separate investigating wing if necessary.

Corruption is at the root of every problem in the country. It can be eradicated to a large extent by removing decision making power from individuals. This is possible with digitalization. E-Sevacentres avoided our going to some offices for different kinds of documents. Driving license and the like are made available online. Income tax assessments for most of the people are settled online without human intervention. Still human decision making is necessary at higher levels. We need effective vigilance by authorized forces.

Casteism and regionalism have been major hurdles in the development of our country. Political parties select candidates based on caste strength in the constituency. Some people vote based on their castes. So some inefficient people or criminals are getting elected. Governments distribute ministries maintaining caste and regional balance giving a go bye to merit of the elected representatives. In a way parties and politicians are perpetuating this malady without giving scope for meritorious people to come to governance.

The Bhagavad Gita says: Every person has to do his duty. Unfortunately, in our society, everybody talks about rights, but nobody talks about duties. We want freedom to talk, but we do not bother whether we are speaking truth and are doing the right thing. We want to do what we like, but never care to see if it hurts anyone. If everyone does his duty, there need not be supervisors, police or judiciary. Progress of the country will be automatic, and consequently individuals will be benefited. Once a boss, instead of asking his employees to do the maximum, asked them to do the minimum thereby suggesting that they are not doing even the minimum expected of them. Our progress depends on our efficiency and dedication to work.

Education is the root to development. Improper education leads to inefficient people in all fields who spoil everything they do. Well supervised education creates efficient people and leads to research which in turn leads to innovation. Innovations are used by industry to produce wealth. More innovations get more industries and more employment for people. Thus, education is the royal route to development.

The British treated us as half-naked snake charmers and felt "Whiteman's burden" to civilize us. They not only enslaved our country, but also enslaved our minds by introducing English education, due to which we lost our touch with Sanskrit in which our cultural heritage had been stored. With the material prosperity based on science, the West became a model for us. We should not forget our great past which exists even today in the form of some beneficial customs and traditions. But basking in our past glory does not fill our stomach today. So we have to be conscious of our roots. But at the same time we should be open minded to receive good from all corners of the world for our progress.

India has been one culturally. Though politically there had been many kingdoms in the past. The British made us a colony of their empire. And their divide-and-rule policy made us conscious of the importance of unity, and we fought to become one independent nation. But even today we see some jealous, back-stabbing people who are seeking help from enemy countries and organizations to gain power. They are encouraging and supporting even anti-national forces and sowing seeds of intolerance among different sections of our society. Governments should take effective steps, and public must help governments in rooting out criminals.

Our economic policy changed from 'License Raj' to 'Market Economy.' Encouraging private enterprise is the order of the day. But in a county like India, big businessmen create syndicates to raise prices. Public Sector is also necessary to control syndicates. Visualizing this, our past policy makers adopted 'Mixed Economy' in which both—Public and Private sectors thrive. If Public Sector does not function well, it should be set right. We don't burn our house because there are rats in it.

Let us believe that we will be able to achieve much in the coming years and make India a better nation in which people live safely, comfortably and happily. May our country be better like this!

(Courtesy: Prof. Rajendra Singh Baisthakur, M. Phil, PGDTE, Senior Lecturer in English (Retd.), Visvodaya Govt. Degree College, Venkatagiri, Balaji, A.P.)

21
Views on Different Issues

On Enforcement Directorate

On actions being taken so rashly by the Enforcement Directorate, ShriAshutosh Kumar says clearly that it is disgusting to see a respectable agency like the Enforcement Directorate being used to muzzle the opposition leaders. The ED does not go after even a local BJP leader. If this is how it goes, the respect for central agency will come down. They have started unleashing terror on opposition leaders to cover up their multiple failures like unemployment, skyrocketing prices of essential commodities such as oil and gas and a lot more. There is a mounting deficit in the revenue receipts which may put the government on the mat.

The concerted drive by the ED in different states has raised furors and aggrieved parties are accusing the BJP of political vendetta. While dubious transactions are being operated, they should be exposed, but it is the lethargy of investigating agencies that gives room to needless controversies.

On Caste Based Census

Caste based census should not be encouraged in India. Certain political parties are aiming to build their vote banks trough caste based census. A sheer reality is that caste census will not help remove the social inequalities in Hindustan. I feel that caste based political outfits should be banned.

Reservation should be based only on the economic status of a person, and not on the basis of his caste. The union government should restrict states from holding caste based census.

One may say that this is a smart play on the part of our government. One may say that it is counter punch diplomacy. But it is effective only in a country where it is held in high esteem and displays strategic clarity. India's diplomatic maturity has given us recognition like never before. The world is taking us seriously.

Views on the Jobs

Creation of maximum jobs should have been the prime focus of the Central as well state governments. But it is not going so. We wasted eight years. We are using our social and political capital to divide the people of India achieving nothing and nothing till date.

Empowerment of Youth and Women

Empowering women and youth plays a crucial role in the development of the society. An empowered woman reduces the gender disparity. She leads to equality of men in the society. ShriAshutosh believes that motivation can help individuals empower them and take positive changes in their lives. The RJJP aims to empower the girl child and women by continuing their education and helping them achieve bigger dreams.

Women continue to experience barriers in almost every aspect of economic life. Women suffer from persistent social and cultural discrimination and unequal access to and control over assets and services. Gender equality may be promoted by increasing opportunities for both girls and boys. Youth and women should be a part of the process which leads to change. They have the energy and time to continue the work for many more years.

I think many young women hesitate to talk about gender issues or gender equality because they are afraid to be called bossy or feminist. Personally, I would try to encourage them to bring this issue on the table. Gender equality must not be considered as a theme that would force men to give things up, but to plan how to get more things.

I don't know that how many of you would agree or disagree, but despite living in the most advanced era, we still have the young generation with stereotype thinking. We need to change that by teaching them that we need a progressive world with the women by our sides. Men must help women, and women must help other women in progressing towards women's economic empowerment.

Youths need to understand the importance of women empowerment in the society. The youths have the power to create a change. And with the help of organizations, who work with women and girls, a society with gender equality can be attained. Trainings and workshop should be set up to encourage financial freedom and security of women. Also, the need to fight with voices, not violence, must be established to ensure a peaceful society. As a leader of the youth in the state of Bihar and several other outermost areas, I feel that there are many ways in which we can contribute to women's empowerment.

The use of social media has made it easier for the youth to voice their views and opinions on the need for gender equality. The UN also recognizes that youth have a crucial role in effecting positive changes by organizing social protests and social media campaigns. So organizing youth to speak and to be heard is necessary. The other thing is to stimulate and guarantee their participation in regional, national, international discussions, and also guarantee that they're being listened to by policy makers.

The UN's women empowerment principles empower women in the workplace, marketplace and community. They have proven to be effective. We should be encouraging our companies and businesses to sign the statement that would signal their support for gender equality.

He (Ashutosh Kumar) agrees that today's youth can contribute greatly to women's empowerment. It starts, though, by creating awareness or educating them about some of the issues or challenges that women face. Change begins with education. Some of the barriers to the empowerment of women are ingrained in cultural and societal norms that hinder progress and it does not help if youth are exposed to the same social norms and expectations that hinder women. Youth should understand the barriers to women such as—sexual harassment, unfair hiring, unequal pay, career blocks, etc. Let the youth decide how they can create change.

Violence against women is also another issue that youth can also prevent. A lot of recommendations can also be applied to women's empowerment such as the use of social media, critical thinking, education, literacy, and reflection, etc.

22

Views on the Minorities

The concept of minority is all clear. A considerable size of lesser population in a particular religion or community is deemed to be the minority. In other words, minorities are always lesser in population than those of the other community of people. Minorities are all at national, cultural, ethnic, religious and linguistic bases. The minority status has been recognized by Central or state governments by certain legislations, or by internationally binding declarations.

Every right granted to the minority is a privilege unavailable to the majority. The minority is set apart from the rest. Minorities are given what is taken away from the majority. The majority's loss is the minority's gain. This seems to be a bit unfair because it creates a blatant inequality between the two. But it is essential for national integration and as for self-respect.

Minority rights are based on the recognition that minorities are in a vulnerable situation in comparison to other groups in society, namely the majority population. We aim to protect members of a minority group from discrimination, assimilation, prosecution, hostility or violence as a consequence of their status. It should be highlighted that minority rights do not constitute privileges, but act to ensure equal respect for members of different communities. These rights serve to accommodate vulnerable groups and to bring all members of society to a minimum level of equality in the exercise of their human and fundamental rights.

The protection of minorities is essential to the stability. It is essential for democratic security and maintenance of peace in this country. A pluralist and democratic society should not only respect the ethnic, cultural, linguistic and religious identity of each person belonging to minority, but also create appropriate conditions enabling them to express, preserve and develop this identity. Creation of a climate of tolerance and dialogue is necessary to enable cultural diversity to be a source and a factor, not of division, but of enrichment for each society.

Minorities require special measures to ensure that they benefit from the same rights as the rest of the population. Hence, minority rights serve to bring all members of society to a balanced enjoyment of their human rights. In other words, their aim is to ensure that persons belonging to a national minority enjoy equality with those persons belonging to the majority. In this context, the promotion of equal opportunities at all levels for people belonging to a national minority is particularly important, since it empowers communities and promotes the exercise of individual freedoms.

Rights of minorities are the protection of their identity. Promoting and protecting their identity prevents forced assimilation and the loss of cultures, religions and languages.

Minority rights are about ensuring respect for distinctive identities. Positive action is required to respect cultural, religious and linguistic diversity. Minorities enrich society through this diversity.

The protection of minority rights is an exercise of tolerance and inter-cultural dialogue. By encouraging mutual respect and understanding, the different groups that comprise a society should be able to engage and cooperate with one another. The basic elements required for the realization of this goal are to promote knowledge of minorities' culture, history, language and religion in an intercultural perspective. In other words, the protection of minority's rights can promote an inclusive, peaceful and prosperous democratic society.

United Nations Declaration on the Rights of Minorities: The United Nations require states to protect the existence and identities of minorities. It also calls upon states to encourage the promotion of ethnic, cultural, religious and linguistic identities. Under Article 2 (1) of this Declaration, minorities shall have the right to practice their religion, enjoy their culture and use their own language in both public and private settings without any kind of discrimination. Article

3 of this Declaration guarantees persons belonging to minorities the right to exercise their rights individually without discrimination. It was adopted by the General Assembly resolution 47/135 on 18 December, 1992.

We would like to ensure full membership in society, equal opportunities and equal treatment for all. Accessing public goods and services should be guiding principles when developing integration policies. This means that States have to proactively promote diversity and create conditions for everyone to feel like and act as full members of that society.

International standards recognize the important role of political parties in promotion of tolerance, cultural diversity and resolution of questions related to minorities. Politicians must play an essential role in the process of integration—both as legislators and decision makers. The RJJP is committed to take efforts to ensuring full rights of the minorities if comes in power or at least sits in the opposition.

23

Thoughts on the Downtrodden

ShriAshutosh opens his mind and sets his thoughts on the downtrodden. His views are all clear. He speaks as such:

"By downtrodden, we simply mean an individual or a group of family who is oppressed, deprived or humiliated. A downtrodden is he who had been kept down by the rulers, mostly belonging to the castes other than the *Savarnas,* in a specific time and particular situation. He is subjugated, tyrannized and persecuted by those who had got powers or authority. A downtrodden is a person who is facing a grievousness, deprivation and paucity. He is subjected to humiliation. He is socially isolated at the hands of the shrewd politicians and other so-called lower or middle clan of people. They (the downtrodden) are exploited since long and this creation is manmade." Ashutosh says: "Men of all nations, castes, races, colours are made of the same soil created by the supreme power. It is the man himself who had created barriers among themselves. All castes are equal. Their existence is inevitable. They are beautiful creations of God."

The important reason behind this heresy is social disrespect shown to them by rich persons of so-called backward class society. The castes feeling in the minds of the people are more harmful than the open abuses showered on them. The reservation given to the downtrodden is discriminatory. It does not benefit the needy. Steps are to be taken to reach the benefits to the really needy people. The comparatively rich and happy people belonging to the SC/ST/OBC are hindrances to their uplift. This should be taken care of.

The downtrodden is considered a set of castes living peacefully. They are persistently labouring hard. They occupy an important role in terms of service to society and the development of country. Down from the ancient times, they were addressed like Shudras. During twentieth century Mahatma Gandhi addressed them like Harijans. But presently, they have accepted themselves to be addressed like Dalits. "Dalit" is the word the lowered community has taken for themselves. They refused to accept Harijans or untouchables.

In this context, Ashutosh further clears: "In fact, Dalit is not a caste. It is a constructed identity which is comprehensive. This term comprises of only the scheduled castes and scheduled tribes. They are long suppressed into submission and silence. They are marginalized. They emerged out of the shadow of centuries of subjugation. We should take more care of them. The RJJP is committed to.

24

Caste Based Reservation

On the issue of the caste based reservation ShriAshutosh Kumar speaks from the core of his heart and says clearly that caste based reservation should be abolished altogether. But self-esteem of the downtrodden is to be maintained. Their share must go to them and not to the reach people of their community. Let the non-deserving people get away from benefits of reservation so that the less privileged and the downtrodden may get the benefits of reservation. This must continue till they are socially free and enjoy their equal rights and freedom in society.

A large group of people who is socially developed and economically strong is shamelessly exploiting the benefits of reservation which are meant for the uneducated downtrodden classes of people. They are a curse to their own society. Such people should be recognized, counted and thrown out of the parameter of reserved categories of people.

Ashutosh puts a narration from *The Expression:* An International Multidisciplinary–e-journal (A Peer Reviewed and indexed Journal with Impact Factor 1.84, ISSN-2395-4132) that says:

India is a country which has a large class of folks without a leader. And, this class comprises over twenty percent of total population. This class is none other than the downtrodden class. These people are divided, disunited, fragmented and broken into various sub-groups based on the intra-caste differences. They are politically exploited and humiliated which is another important cause of maintaining this class difference. They are deprived of their rights and could not get what they deserve. The upper class socially thinks all this and wants to soothe out. There should be concerted efforts by the downtrodden to mobilize fund and spend the same for its economic advancement. Upper class people should think over these matters to maintain national integrity and communal harmony so that the country would run successfully on the track of prosperity.

The Clause of Article 16 lays down that a citizen on the grounds of religion, race, caste, sex, place of birth or residence cannot be discriminated in respect of any employment of office under the State.

In a case Balaji v/s State of Mysore it was held: "Caste of a person cannot be the sole criteria for ascertaining whether a particular caste is backward or not. Determinants such as poverty, occupation, place of habitation may all be relevant factors to be taken into consideration. The court further said that it does not mean that if once a caste is considered to be backward, it will continue to be backward for all times. The government should review the test and if a clan reaches the state of progress where the reservation is non-necessary, it should delete that class from the list of backward classes."

Thus, the underlying premises of the philosophy of reservation that all members of the backward classes are disadvantaged, while all members of forward castes are deemed to be good enough to administration under their own stream is, in my opinion, not a valid assumption; neither is it fair. Economic condition cannot be ignored when arriving at the decision in our society.

ShriAshutosh says: What is ironical is that even our constitution is reservation friendly. But nowhere in a bare reading of the constitution is the term backward class explicitly defined. What determines or constitutes backwardness, is still unanswered. So the question arises"—how can the reservation be given to backward community for something that is undefined. Actually, they are enjoying ghee and butter hiding their face in a big black blanket day and night slapping in the face of their own categories of people. This picture is to be erased from our society. They are to be made exempted of all reservations.

Caste based reservation policy fails to recognize social backwardness. With increasing globalization and urbanization, caste loyalties are weakening and hence new parameters defining social backwardness need to be identified. Reservation should explicitly include economic criteria. The person having financial security should not be given any reservation. Reservation is not for an individual. It is for the community. A rich person, irrespective of caste can access and afford education of his children and does not need the protection by the reservation policy. It is the poor who need such protection, irrespective of their caste. Everyone should be given an equal opportunity to prove their worth. No section of society should be spoon fed. Instead, they should be provided with adequate sources. And at the end, merit should prevail.

Castes are mainly used by politicians for their vote banks. This term is only effective in government offices. On 1st April 2012, Sri Ajay Singh Yadav, a Congress leader from Haryana, amidst controversies on reservation said: Now the time has come to review the caste based reservations. He said that the benefits of reservation should be given to the OBC as well as the general people on the basis of their income.

On September 2008, the Kerala Government has given 7.5 and 10% reservation in respective government colleges and universities. The Muslim Jamat filed a petition in Kerala High Court to challenge his decision. The court decided and expressed that the time has come to come out of the castes based reservation, and to promote it on economic ground. The poor *Savarnas* should also be given the reservation so that they may not face financial hardship due to adverse situation. The court also said that poverty of economic backwardness is the biggest social evil. Now is the time to open competition. The backward clan of people should also think that their progress would be withheld if remains dependent on the government.

Dr. Amit Kumar Verma, Director, Centre for the Study of Society and Politics, Kanpur, expresses his views that caste based reservation should be slowly eliminated. He said no poor should let go only on the basis of his caste. Social justice and representativeness should be given to all poor people, irrespective of their castes.

25

Dilapidating Condition of the Savarnas

"*Savarnas* are people who fall within the caste system but do not practice casteism. They do not believe in the practice of untouchability as well. *The Savarnas*do not conform to any caste group to maintain intimate friendship. The large part of population of *Savarnas* does not propose discrimination in any form in the daily interactions with anybody. They neither ask for nor care about the caste or religion of a person while making a day to day dealing. They truthfully participate in all societal functions. They are at par with other residents. Where do you see the sense of discrimination in society except in employment in government offices? In fact, there is no way to know the caste of a person unless he advertises the same. *Savarnas*interact with anyone, no problem. They think that Brahmin woman working in the corporate world is no longer a Brahmin, but a worker. Likewise, a Dalit working in any institutionis no longer a Dalit, but an ordinary worker. The Constitution of India provides equal rights to all citizens; a lot more to the oppressed sections of society. But for decades, the social and economical condition of the *Savarnas* is dilapidating. They are being devoid of equal rights and opportunities. This situation should be taken care of.

The *Ambedkarite*agenda of emancipation is a big issue of concern that must be addressed to. I have been in many conversations to my fellow *Ambedkarites* where they have maintained that the *Savarna* is the best category of people. *Savarnas*have not knowingly done anything bad to other sections of society. They always do good deeds. But alas! They presently fall in the most dilapidating condition. They are hard of money to meet even their most essential needs. They are starving. Essential things are scarce to them. Even their livelihood is rolled upon. They are left to their own destiny. They are habitually ignored by the people in power. They are ill treated from every corner.

Every social or political move goes against them. The government must take care of this situation before it is too late"—Ashutosh expresses.

26
Menace of Dowry

ShriAshutosh sees the system of dowry for marriage as a curse to our society. The socially declared mandatory giving and taking of dowry for marriage is still kicking in incredible India. The facts remain that despite changes in the law; growing awareness of it; more educational and economical progress, women are bought and sold for a price under the institution of marriage. Dowry has not disappeared. It has morphed. He refers to the SeemaRohini's narration. SeemaRohini, in her interesting and relevant book *Sita's Curse, Stories of Dowry Victims* (HarperCollins, 2003), gives a humorous yet apt description of dowry as it has come to be today—

"Dowry has become a bribe paid to a husband to keep the wife's body and soul together. A woman is a mere conduit to a good dowry—the definition of good being flexible and expandable. The boys are on sale and there is no discount in the marriage market. There is no "buy one, get one free" here. It is a transaction weighted against the woman. In fact, it is a sale where even after the price is paid, satisfaction is not guaranteed. And ironically, the sales never complete with marriage. The buyer is expected to keep paying in cash and to be kind during festivals to celebrate child birth, and to mark ritualistic occasion. Any excuse is good enough to keep the way moving with gifts."

The practice of dowry is a very crucial question to be answered by decent civil society. In the present society, a large number of parents are not able to pay the huge amount of money as dowry which they are asking for marriage. In this situation, parents are forced to search alternatives to meet their needs. Even after the marriage, these girls are facing severe kind of threats from their families. Sometimes this leads to mental depression of the girls, alienation in the family and in society, separation from husband, and ultimately—the suicide. The value of girls is very precious; that is more than the dowry. But in the present society, nobody understands that value even if there are numerous laws and policies or the dowry. The threats of dowry are largely eating the life of the women. We, being the responsible, should address this issue positively.

27
Azadi Ka Amrit Mahotsav

AzadiKaAmritMahotsav is an initiative of the government of India. It is to celebrate and commemorate the 75th years of independence of glorious history of the people, their culture and achievements. It means elixir of energy of independence, elixir of inspiration of the warriors of freedom struggle, elixir of new ideas, and elixir of *Aatmanirbhar Bharat*. The method is awakening of the nation and festival of fulfilling the dreams of new government. It is the idea of increasing nationalism, patriotism and celebrating historic milestone of independence as by discussion and debate in the whole country.

HarGharTiranga is a different move to make people aware of freedom struggle. It is to create patriotism in the countrymen. When they hold the flag, their heads hold high. The flag tells us to be ever alert, be ever on the move, go forward, and work for a free, flexible, compassionate, decent and democratic society.

"But we see darkness glooming all around. The whole country is at high fall. There is a fall of money value. There is a rapid depreciation of rupees as against dollars. There is a trade deficit. There is an outflow of capital. There is an acute fall in foreign reserves with the RBI. Nothing expected happened as yet. Deterioration is everywhere. Unemployment is at high spark. Economy is almost on a big slop. Discontent is rife. The whole country's economy is likely to blast. Their bad and teasing policy like *Pakodanomics* is resulting in unemployment increase. The policy is surely making a mockery of the unemployed youth. Who is responsible for all this?"—Ashutosh asks on behalf of the people of India.

How can a citizen celebrate and enjoy the *AmritMahotsav* as asked humourously to do so? This is nothing but an act of sheer foolishness to participate in such a humourousprogramme being an attempt to befool our citizens", Ashutosh says.

The current period, we are living in, is frivolously declared as *"AmritKaal"* by doubtful political pundits of their own design. And the countrymen are asked to observe and celebrate *"AmritMahotsav"* in the time of acute pain and grief for the whole nation. The Indian families are really in high peril, but they are blindly pushed into an exaggerating participation of a national ceremony called *AmritMahotsav.* Ashutosh says: This is a cynical act of befooling our country. This is nothing but an indication of likely dilapidation of the Indian economy, the whole countrymen will suffer. What an irony of Indian nationals! The whole citizens are stunned, startled, dazed, dazzled, bewildered and flabbergasted. This is a newly created reckless design of detrimental nationalism India are tracking on.

28

Agnipath Scheme

The government of India launched a historical and revolutionary recruitment scheme for Indian youth to serve in the Armed Forces by the name *Agnipath.* The youth enrolled under the *Agnipath Scheme* will be known as *Agniveers.* It is a new scheme of self-styled government to recruit the Indian youth who wish to join the Armed Forces wherein the selected candidates will be enrolled as *Agniveers*for a period of four years. It is a recruitment process of individuals below the rank of officer, with the goal of deploying fitter, electrician, light man and other lower level posts, along with younger troops on the front lines. Many of them will be on four-year contracts. It is said to be a game changing project that will give the Indian Army, Indian Navy, and the Indian Air Force a young and youthful image.

The government overconfidently says that the *Agnipath Scheme* is aimed at fundamentally changing the way that sailors, airmen and soldiers are recruited. But for many people joining the armed forces is more a passion than an avocation.

The scheme raises many questions: In that shortened training, is it sufficient to equip a soldier for modern warfare? Will *Agniveer* be as motivated as permanent soldier? Will the two different categories of soldiers respect the unity and solidarity of the armed forces at the same length?

Ashutosh thinks thrice and enumerates the idea of T. N. Venugopalan, Kochi, Kerala that this government should use the first *Agniveer*as a test run before going ahead with full fledged implementation of the scheme. Or, the tenure should be extended to at least ten years. (published in Frontline, July 29, 2022)Ashutosh being a soldier disapproves this scheme and in his support puts several like-minded views of different army officers:

Major General G. D. Bakshi has defended almost every act of the BJP government. But on the *Agniveer* scheme he seems to have given no consent. He wrote in his tweet:

> *"Was flabbergasted by the Agniveer scheme. I thought initially it was a trial being done on a pilot basis. This is an across the board change to convert Indian armed forces to a short tenure quasi-conscript force like the Chinese. For God's sake PLEASE DON'T do it."*

Lieutenant General Vinod Bhatia, Paratrooper and former Director General of Military Operations, spoke to the media and made his opposition to the move clear:

> *"On ToD [Tour of Duty], pray & hope that Agnipath succeeds, for the sake of nation, armed forces and the Agniveers. The government will need to take the ownership and ensure it succeeds as the process is irreversible and high risk." Later he told an Internet-based television channel: "I am a paratrooper, I take risks, but this is not a risk I would've taken; the Fauj ethos may change."*

Lieutenant General Raj Kadyan, former Vice Chief of the Army Staff, had opposed themove when he was in service. He expresses his views on an Internet based channel:

> *"This kind of scheme should be tried out in a low risk organization. We are trying it out in the defense forces, where the risk is very high... I only hope and pray that there is no war. If there's [going to be] a war, you don't expect a man who is already looking beyond four years to be committed to the extent that he can lay down his life."*

B. N. Sharma, former Chief Instructor, BSF Academy, who has served in almost all the high insurgency areas in the Northeast, wrote on Twitter:

"To me Agnipath scheme looks like a scheme for any newly launched security agency; assuring contract for four years and extension of contract for only twenty five per cent."

In a nutshell, Ashutosh says that this scheme seems detrimental to the vigour of the Indian Armed forces.

29

Youth Unemployment

Unemployment is defined as absence of suitable vocation for employable skilled person. In India It is increasing day in day out. Youth unrest is rife. We must seek solution from our government because it is the main river of employment. Demonetization, faulty GST implementation, and afterwards a severe lockdown throughout the country destroyed everything whatever it was. We fail to find any clue to why economy is going down. Jobs are not there. Exports are only a little more than nil. Everybody on the street knows the truth except our political giants.

Unemployment today stands as a big problem. It is a curse. But we can endeavour to overcome it a long way with consistent efforts, patience and perseverance. Thoughts of ShriAshutosh Kumar on increasing unemployment are consented upon the few following lines we should pay attention to:

The education system of India needs to be reformed to address the bitter increase in unemployment. The emphasis on education should shift from theory. Agricultural activities should be diversified into fisheries.

A blind course of action being taken for the privatization of government establishments, such as the railways, Public Sector Undertakings, government companies and other important installations should be undone. This is a coal black course of mindless action. This seems to be a willful attempt to conspire against the unemployed youth of India.

Just to create opportunities of employment and engage our youth at most, we should try to establish more industries where young people could be employed with gaining profit. We have to reduce the cost of the products. We should keep on doing some more innovations so that when new product is launched, people should purchase it again, and the process of selling and buying keeps on going.

If the person is not educated up to the level that he can get good job, then there should be some opportunity to learn skills by which he can initiate a start-up for self-employment.

Agriculture should be given high priority in the country where agricultural climate is good so that more and more youths should attract to agriculture and agro-based industries. Because of good productivity of food, the cost of livelihood will be reduced. Farmers should be given facilities and knowledge as and when required at very low cost. They should be provided seeds, fertilizers and electricity at highly subsidized rate.

There should be good medical systems at low fees so that youths should not hesitate to visit hospitals. Jobs in medical field should also be increased this way.

Every youth should be taught internet skills so that he can learn some easy skills without paying for trainings.

If good transport facilities are provided at low cost, this inspires people to transport their products to remote areas and earn a good value for them. This will help employability. There are many such kinds of innovation required which will surely reduce employment.

Further, Ashutosh says: "Honesty, loyalty, perseverance, inspiration, motivation and faith in God are always required." We should keep belief in.